THE CURIOUS GOURMAND

ANTOINE MELON

Copyright © 2024 by Antoine Melon

All rights reserved. This book or any portion thereof may not be reproduced or used in any manner whatsoever without the express written permission of the publisher, except for the use of brief quotations in a book review.

Table of Contents

Preface	1
Absinthe	3
Aioli	5
Alcohol | Aperitif | Eau de Vie | Liqueur | Liquor | Spirit	7
Amuse-Bouche | Canapés | Petits Fours | Mignardises	9
Andres Carne de Res	11
Apicius	13
Aquavit	15
Assassin	17
Baba	18
Bain-Marie	20
Beaujolais Nouveau	22
Bellini	24
Bibendum	26
Big Apple	28
Biscuit | Afternoon Tea	30
Bloody Mary	32
Bocuse D'Or	34
Bouchon	36
Bouillabaisse	38
Boxing Day	40
Brunch	42
Bûche de Noël	44
Cacao Beans	46
Caesar Salad	48
Carat	50

Carbonara	52
Carnival	54
Carpaccio	56
Catty & Tael	58
Club des Chefs des Chefs	59
Châteauneuf Du Pape	61
Châteaux of Bordeaux	63
Chilies	66
Chin Chin	68
Chocolate Cookies	70
Chopsticks	72
Chowder	74
Cocido	76
Cocktail	78
Coffee	81
Cordon Bleu	83
Cosmopolitan	85
Crêpes Suzette	87
Croissant	89
Croque-Monsieur	91
Crying Onion	93
Dai Pai Dong	95
Daube of Beef	97
Dim Sum	99
Dom Perignon | Dom Ruinart | La Grande Dame | Cristal Roederer	101
Dragon Beard Candy	104
Dudu	106
Easter Egg	108
Finger Tapping	110
Forbidden Fruit	112

The Fork	114
French 75	116
French Fries	118
Galette des Rois & The King's Cake	120
Gazpacho	122
Grog	124
Hainan Chicken	126
Hamburger	128
Herbs of Provence	130
Honeymoon	132
HP Sauce	134
Indian Tonic Water	136
John Dory	138
Karkade	140
Kellogg's / Liebig - The Physicians	142
Kir	144
The Knife	146
Kosher	148
Kugelhopf	150
Laguiole	152
Laureate	154
Lavender, Rosemary, Tarragon, Sage & Basil	156
Le Creuset / Staub	158
Lord & Lady	160
Macaroons	162
Madeleine	164
Melon	166
Mère Brazier	168
MOF	170
Mortadella	172

Morue	174
Moscow Mule | Blood & Sand | Screwdriver By Eben Freeman	176
Note a Note	178
Opera / Éclair / Sarchertorte / Paris Brest Pastries	180
Oreo	182
Ortolan	184
Oscar Tschirsky Waldorf Salad | Egg Benedict | Thousand Island Dressing	186
Oysters & Pearls	188
Pacojet	190
Paella	192
Pastis	194
Peach Melba & Pear Belle Hélène	196
Personalities	198
Pistou / Pesto	207
Pizza	209
Pomme Purée	211
Pomodoro	213
Popcorn	215
Pretzel	217
Raised Finger	219
Ratatouille	220
Red Bull	222
Rolling Stones	224
Rollmops	226
Salary	228
Sauerkraut	230
Service	232

Shark's Fin	234
Sidecar & Margarita	236
Singapore Sling	238
Sot l'y laisse Chicken Oysters	240
Spam	242
Steak Tartare I Bistro	244
Stollen	246
Swiss Chocolate	248
Table Superstitions	250
Tapas	252
Tapenade	254
Tarte Tatin	256
Tempura	258
Thousand-Year-Old Egg	260
Toque Blanche	262
Trou Normand	264
Turkey	266
Turkish Delight	268
Valentine's Chocolate	270
Vatel & Chantilly	272
Wellington	274
Winebottle Trivia	276
You Are What You Eat	278
Bibliography	280
General Bibliography	288

Preface

Paul Bocuse once gave me a car.

It was a toy car, of course, but I loved it as if it were life-sized. The date was 3 November 1979, my seventh birthday. Like true Lyonnais, my parents chose to mark the occasion with food, at Bocuse's celebrated restaurant, L'Auberge du Pont de Collonges. That day I had Bocuse's signature truffle soup V.G.E. (named after Valerie Giscard d'Estaing, who was president at the time), and then ate sea bass stuffed with lobster mousse in puff pastry with Sauce Choron. I finished with a vanilla île flottante (a 'Floating Island'), while one of Bocuse's staff, wearing a red uniform trimmed with gold braid and brass buttons, played an Orjels-Winn barrel organ. My family sang "*Bon anniversaire, nos voeux les plus sincères…*"

But the dinner's most impressive moment happened when Monsieur Paul himself came to our table; he was wearing his whites, while his chef's hat made him the tallest man I had ever seen. That was when he offered me a miniature version of his own 1972 Citroën Dyane. That little car bore all the region's finest meats, cheeses, fruits and vegetables, from Lyons' famous market, Les Halles, to L'Auberge du Pont du Collonges.

From that moment on, I wanted a life based around food and artists like Monsieur Paul. That meal actually changed my destiny, which would otherwise have been to take over Maison Melon, a jewellery house that my great-great-grandfather Jean-Pierre Melon founded in 1850.

I am grateful to the many people who helped create this book.

First, I wish to thank my parents, Pierre and Christiane Melon, for teaching me at an early age to appreciate good food; they always took me to restaurants of all kinds. Thank you also for sending me to the world's most prestigious hotel management school, Switzerland's l'École Hotelière de Lausanne.

I also owe much to my teachers at Lausanne, in particular Chef Vladimir Durussel, or Dudu, as we students knew him. Dudu was the first to instil in me a passion for culinary history, which gave rise to this book.

Throughout my career, I have been privileged to meet many of the greatest chefs of our era: Paul Bocuse, Pierre Gagnaire, Joël Robuchon, Ferran Adrià, Daniel Boulud, Michel Bras, Martin Berasategui, Jordi Roca, Oriol Balaguer, Thomas Keller, Heston Blumenthal, Marco Pierre White, and many more. Their work has inspired me to come up with my own recipe, *The Curious Gourmand*.

I really hope that you will enjoy reading *The Curious Gourmand* as much as I enjoyed writing it. You will find here personal anecdotes as well as the origins of certain dishes, beverages, cocktails and customs. Over the last twenty-five years, I have lived and worked in more than ten countries; I have tried to collect culinary stories here from my travels.

Thanks also to my deceased grandmother, Petite Mamie, who shared her cooking insights, many of which are recorded here.

I would like to thank the many friends who shared their knowledge and stories – if what you've told me isn't here, look for your tale in my next book!

Many of the anecdotes I recount are urban legends; others are historical facts. You will discover the literal meaning for dim sum, the origins of the hamburger, the story of the Bloody Mary, and how the word carat unites the jeweller's world with the cooks.

Bon Appétit!

Absinthe

For me absinthe is synonymous with the Belle Époque, when painters and writers evoked its heady effects in their art. You can almost see its vapours swirling in the paintings of Van Gogh, or in the Art Nouveau designs of Toulouse-Lautrec. Other famous drinkers included Oscar Wilde and Paul Verlaine. Degas caused a scandal when he painted a woman sipping absinthe. Ernest Hemingway created a cocktail combining it with Champagne and named it Death in the Afternoon. But while it was credited in Paris's bohemian circles for releasing the creative spirit, a darker reputation for causing violence and even madness emerged. By 1915 "absinthism" was denounced as a debilitating condition and a threat to society, and the drink was banned in France.

Absinthe is a spirit made from the distillation of herbs, flowers and leaves, including *Artemisia absinthium*, or wormwood, which gave its name to the beverage as well as its characteristic bitter, anise flavour. It is a compound in the wormwood called thujone that was blamed (and celebrated!) for absinthe's hallucinatory effects. The traditional manner of serving it is to place a sugar cube on a special slotted spoon over a glass containing a small measure of it and then pour water drop by drop over the sugar cube to gently release its aroma. The botanicals give the undiluted spirit a green colour and preparing it in this way turns it milky white, hence a few of its aliases: the Green Fairy, the Emerald Hell (before); the White Lady, Opaline.

I first tried absinthe when my friend Nicolas Payet, who worked for Pernod Ricard, brought a bottle to the house we shared near Putney

Bridge in London. Pernod Fils was one of the original distillers and turned its production over to the similar, wormwood-free pastis after the ban. Never as popular (and therefore never as troublesome!) in the United Kingdom as on the continent, it had escaped the ban and by the late 1990s was being rediscovered by connoisseurs and curious drinkers.

We stared at the bottle, wondering how much we should pour. We were expecting some sort of transfiguration, although we did get spectacularly drunk. It is now known that the tiny amount of thujone in absinthe isn't psychoactive at all; perhaps its famous effects can instead be attributed to a combination of its very high alcohol content and artistic exaggeration.

With absinthe enjoying a revival in Britain and other European countries where it had never been prohibited, France lifted the ban and production began once more. Now it can be found in trendy bars around the world, which are rediscovering old cocktail recipes such as the pre-ban Sazerac from New Orleans, which combines it with rye whiskey and bitters. In London you can find it at Opium bar in Chinatown.

So, you don't have to be a brilliant artist to drink absinthe!

Recipe:

Death in the Afternoon

http://absinthehour.com/category/absinthe-recipes/

Restaurant | Famous Chef:

Absinthe Brasserie & Bar, San Francisco

http://www.absinthe.com/

Aioli

Though I have travelled and worked all over the world, Provence remains my spiritual home. I am from Lyons, but like the Impressionists I was drawn to this region of France for its light, its habits (*see Pastis*) and its food full of flavours. The little towns of Eygalières, Cassis, St Rémy de Provence, Gordes, Cucuron, Lacoste, Aix, Maussane les Alpilles, St Paul de Vence: however far away I am, they never leave me. My parents live in Eygalières, and for me no visit home is complete without a trip to the market. I love Provence's globe artichokes; the delicate green tiny artichokes, *violets de Provence*, which you can eat almost without cooking; the tomatoes in all their dodgy shapes and irregular colours, which I find infinitely preferable to the often boring and tasteless supermarket varieties.

If there is a dish that can typify this vibrant region, it must be Le Grand Aioli, in which its delicious produce and fish adorn a bowl of this redolent sauce.

Aioli comes from the Occitan word *alholi*, meaning garlic and oil. The recipe is simple: using a mortar and pestle, first crush the garlic, add an egg yolk and then, while mixing, slowly add the olive oil to obtain a similar consistency to mayonnaise. This process is called emulsion: you use an emulsifier, (egg yolk), to mix two otherwise unblendable substances (olive oil and the garlic juice).

Aioli is famous for accompanying salted cod (see *morue*), raw vegetables, hard boiled eggs or fish soup, but is also delicious simply spread over some croutons. Its popularity is not limited to Provence;

in Spain it is enjoyed with paella, and in Italy with grilled meats and fish. Regional variations include the addition of mustard, olive oil and saffron, to name a few, but my preference is for the original, as served at my wedding buffet in Mausanne les Alpilles!

At the banquet everything came from artisanal Provençal farmers and craftsmen. We had one long, long table, just like the Sicilian wedding in *The Godfather*. We served aioli and tapenade, and Sisteron lamb, whose flesh tastes salty because the sheep lick the Provençal stones, which have high saline content. We ate eggplant browned in olive oil; plates of charcuterie; and a pyramid of macaroons. Unfortunately the marriage did not last but the memory of the buffet remains.

A word to the wise: don't forget to brush your teeth after eating aioli!

Recipe:

Aioli recipe from J-Y de Moro

jy.de.moro@wanadoo.fr

Restaurant | Famous Chef:

Jean-Yves de Moro caterer, Saint Martin de Crau

http://www.pageswebpro-alimentaire.com/bouches-du-rhone/boulangerie-et-boulangerie-patisserie/de-moro-sa_f231545

Alcohol | Aperitif | Eau de Vie | Liqueur | Liquor | Spirit

You never forget the first time you're drunk, however much you might want to, afterward. I first drank gin and orange, and I can promise that I have never touched that particular mixture again. Unfortunately, such youthful indiscretions result in a long list of cocktails that are untouchable forever afterward because of their unpleasant associations!

Have you ever wondered why distilled alcohol is classified as a "spirit", which normally refers either to the soul or a supernatural being?

The word 'alcohol' comes from the Arabic *al-kuhl,* meaning "the kohl," the fine black powder used in ancient times as both an antiseptic and eyeliner. It was originally produced by refining the mineral stibnite to obtain the quintessence ("spirit") of the substance. The word alcohol passed into English to mean all distilled liquids, eventually referring commonly to ethanol (the alcohol found in drinks) in the eighteenth century.

During the Middle Ages, it was believed that demonic possession was responsible for the effects of alcohol – the loss of balance, the babbling, laughter or tears. Drunkenness was explained by a "spirit" that took over the drinker's body, provoking devilish behaviour: hence "spirit" came to mean distilled liquor.

Eau-de-vie, a type of spirit distilled from various fruits, of course means "water of life" in French, as the process of distillation was supposedly invented by would-be alchemists as they attempted to create a potion that would result in eternal life or youth. Though those forerunners of Pernod-Ricard fell short of their goal, their efforts were not wasted. Eau-de-vie is usually not aged, resulting in a clear liquor. (An exception is Calvados, the French apple brandy aged in oak casks). Other popular varieties include kirsch, distilled from cherries, Poire William, which is sometimes sold with a whole pear inside the bottle, and *mirabelle*, made from plums.

Liqueur is also an alcoholic beverage flavoured with aromatic substances (fruits, flowers, herbs, spices or even cream); in contrast to spirits, it also includes added sugar. Liqueurs are distinct from liquors as follows: liqueur first refers to a sweetened distilled beverage; meanwhile *liquor* is a more generic term, which refers to any distilled beverage.

Aperitifs should always be served chilled and should stimulate the appetite by quenching thirst. Aperitifs include vermouths (sweet or dry white wine with aromatic herbs), bitters (wine-based drinks with plants and roots) and aniseeds (aniseed drinks).

Dubonnet, the first aperitif, has patriotic origins: the French state held a contest for the best anti-malarial drink to keep their Legionnaires healthy in foreign climes. A chemist called Joseph Dubonnet won the prize: his namesake aperitif muted the bitter dominance of its quinine content, with wine mixed with grape brandy. Dubonnet sweetened and made the drink more complex by adding cinnamon, chamomile, orange peel and green coffee beans to it.

I always knew that alcohol was good for you!

Amuse-Bouche | Canapés | Petits Fours | Mignardises

Most readers will be familiar with these four terms, but many people often get them mixed up with each other.

Before Dinner

Amuse-bouche or amuse-gueule ('mouth amusing') could be translated as 'titbit,' and refers to the savouries offered at the beginning of a meal, before the first course. These small portions are usually not listed on the menu; though small, they offer the chef the chance to show off his virtuosity.

The prudent diner will not eat just anything found on a table. One chef I know (who shall remain nameless) on visiting one of Paris' three-star restaurants (which shall remain nameless), found a brilliant scattering of tiny fruits dappling his tablecloth. He thought they were amuse-bouche; intrigued, he bit into one. Almost immediately he began retching and gasping for air: he was taken to the nearest emergency room in an ambulance. He had accidentally poisoned himself!

The term canapé derives from the eighteenth-century French word for 'sofa' – since these savoury mouthfuls are usually served at cocktail parties balanced on a thin piece of toasted bread. I am particularly fond of the ones offered at the Mandarin Hotel in Macao, Asia's gambling capital:

we served simple cubes from carrots and beets that were cut like dice; the dice were fashioned with a creamy herb mousse. We also had dark chocolate wafers for the 'counters,' which we sprayed with red sugar. At another event when Daniel Boulud visited, we served canapés created to evoke the ancient elements: earth, water, wood, fire, and air. He must have liked the canapés that we served, because he photographed them madly!

After Dinner

Petits fours also comes from the French, in reference to the 'small oven' where little biscuits and cakes were baked in the eighteenth century. Petits fours can be served as savoury (before dinner) or sweet (after). Sometimes the word *bouchée* (mouthful) is also used for small puff pastry vol-au-vent, and tartlets filled with cream.

Mignardises are small pastries served at the end of the meal to accompany coffee or tea. The French adjective *mignarde* means delicate, or pretty. The Fat Duck's Heston Blumenthal is famous for serving a candy bag of 'childhood memories'; in this last little course, he serves edible cards, a pine sherbet fountain with a vanilla dipping stick, an apple pie candy inside an edible wrapper ('Eat All Of Me'), and - pièce de résistance – 'Like A Kid In A Sweet Shop,' an atomizer that creates the nostalgic aroma of liquorice and citrus.

So now you can say you know!

Recipe:	**Restaurant	Famous Chef:**
Sweet Shop recipes	Fat Duck, Heston Blumenthal, Bray
http://www.starchefs.com/features/heston/html/index.shtml	http://www.thefatduck.co.uk/

Andres Carne de Res

I have lived and worked in eleven countries; restaurants are my business. I am sometimes asked whether or not I have a favourite. An elegant Michelin starred place in the classic tradition? Or something more postmodern, that reflects the whimsy of a molecular kitchen? But my answer never fails to surprise: the most amazing restaurant I've ever visited serves barbecue, not *haute cuisine*: it was Andres Carne de Res, in Columbia. The meal I had there was breath-taking. I ate beef tenderloin with a piquant Argentine chimichurri sauce, made of parsley, garlic, olive oil, red pepper, vinegar, paprika, thyme, cumin, oregano, bay leaf, and cilantro.

Andres is located in Chia, about half an hour outside Bogota; the restaurant runs around thousand covers. The logistics are staggering. Outside the restaurant there's a barbecue set up for the drivers and bodyguards. Inside, the restaurant is all glamour, its interior decorated with *brocante*: antiques, old advertisements, vintage machines. The architecture is fascinating: there are cooking areas on different levels, with Heaven (*cielo*) on the top floor, for families, and Hell (*infierno*) on the ground floor, for drinking *aguardiente* and dancing the rumba. Andres is like different houses put together at different heights, with steps zigzagging from one platform to the other. You don't know who staff is, who a customer is; by the end of the evening, everyone is dancing on the tables.

I am passionate about wood fire cooking. There is no better way to be with friends than outdoors on a fine day, chatting while grilling food. I love the flavours of grilled meat and foil-wrapped potatoes roasted among burning coals.

But have you ever thought about the origin of the word *barbecue*? There are two etymologies, though I definitely prefer the first, which would give barbecue a French origin. The word would come from *barbe a queue* ('from beard to tail'), referring to a piglet roasted whole. But the explanation preferred by most linguists traces the English word *barbecue* back through Spanish to the native American Taíno tribe's term *barbacòa* – a green wood rack whose original meaning was 'holy fire pit.' The cooking technique for *barbacòa* involved digging an earthen trench and placing the meat inside to marinate in its own juices; more leaves and coals are placed over the flesh. Then the whole is set ablaze; the meat takes several hours to smoke-cook. Early visitors to the Caribbean record that venison, bear, fish and pumpkin all were cooked over the *barbacòa*; one writer even claimed that the original barbecues made human flesh "savoury."

My new preferred restaurant is Ekstedt in Stockholm, Chef owner Niklas only cooks on wood fire, no electricity no gas used in his cooking. My dream is to bring him to London.

Recipe:

Chimichurri recipe

Restaurant | Famous Chef:

Andres Carnes de Res, Bogota
http://andrescarnederes.com

APICIUS

It was only while researching this book that I came across the first century gourmet and aesthete Marcus Gavius Apicius. Apicius gave his name to the famous Michelin starred restaurant in Paris, previously owned by Chef Jean-Pierre Vigato, whom I came across when I was approached to run the Food and Beverage Department of La Mamounia, the dazzling hotel in Marrakesh.

Apicius is sometimes credited with writing *Ars magirica,* the first Roman cookery book. *Ars magirica* contains the only collection of recipes to survive from classical antiquity. There are only two known extant copies: one is in the Vatican. The other is held in the library of the New York Academy of Medicine, and dates back to the ninth century.

Scholars now believe the attribution of *Ars magirica* to the historical personage Apicius is apocryphal. Because the book was written in a slangy Vulgar Latin rather than in polished classical prose, scholars think that it served as an aide-memoire for kitchen staff. The recipes include recipes for more than 200 sauces and give instructions on making everything from sausages to custards, pies stuffed with "cooked pig teats, fish, chicken, warblers, the bellies of cooked thrushes, 'and all sorts of excellent things' chopped together."

Apicius himself came to a bad end, poisoning himself after his high living and lavish banquets left him bankrupt. He is thus one among several chefs (see *Vatel*) and gourmets who ended their own lives rather than compromise their passion for food.

Those who knew Apicius recounted how his love of food drove him to extremes, whether travelling hundreds of miles to find the sweetest and best prawns (turning around and going home when he found them unsatisfactory) or experimenting with the perfect way to prepare pork livers and flamingo tongues.

Today the word Apicius is a synonym for a gourmet. It also describes a sauce made with red wine vinegar, star anise, cumin seeds, coriander seeds, paprika, curry, soya sauce and some honey: the perfect accompaniment to pork cutlets.

Apicius: inspiration or cautionary tale?

Recipe:

Apicius sauce recipe or recipe from Ars magirica

http://penelope.uchicago.edu/~grout/encyclopaedia_romana/wine/apicius.html

Restaurant | Famous Chef:

Apicius, Jean-Pierre Vigato, Paris

http://www.restaurant-apicius.com/

Aquavit

During my travels I always make a point of trying the local tipples to better understand a country's culture and tastes. For me, trips to Cuba, Scotland, Spain and Sweden simply wouldn't have been complete without sampling the Mojito, single malt whisky, Sangria and Aquavit respectively.

The first thing I noticed in Sweden was that people were drinking a spirit during the meal rather than afterward. The second was that women were knocking it back even more than men!

The word aquavit (or *akvavit*) comes from the Latin meaning "water of life."

Aquavit is a clear or pale-coloured spirit made in Norway, Denmark, Sweden, and northern Germany. Like vodka, aquavit is distilled from fermented potato mash or from fermented grain, before being distilled a second time with herbs, spices and fruit oils, the most prominent flavouring being caraway seeds.

In Sweden, aquavit is drunk at the end of a heavy meal to help digestion; or it may accompany starters like pickled herring, crayfish or smoked fish. Served in a shot glass, aquavit is also often drunk in concert with beer. Tradition recommends that a sip of beer be drunk before or after the aquavit; I even participated in a drinking game that called for dropping the aquavit shot in a pint of beer and putting it away in one go. This is one game to avoid if you are a light drinker: it is a killer. I never won a contest without regretting my success afterward.

According to legend, aquavit helps fish 'to swim down to the stomach,' which could explain its popularity during the crayfish party, (*kräftskiva*). *Kräftskiva* is celebrated throughout Scandinavia in July and August, the traditional end of crayfish harvest.

I have incredible memories of my first *kräftskiva*, which the Swedes look forward to all year. I was in Stockholm with some friends, who took me to Sturehof, a restaurant where waiters still wear white jackets with golden epaulettes. For our *kräftskiva*, we wore silly paper hats, dined off paper tablecloths under paper lanterns; we also had (unfortunately, to my way of thinking) bibs. In the bib I felt as if I were five years old again.

Crayfish are certainly popular in my native Lyons, particularly as the defining ingredient of *sauce Nantua*, but I found the Scandinavian passion for crustaceans to be of a different order of magnitude. The diners fall to their *kräftor*, noisily slurping juices from the crayfish's head *before* eating the meat. And I have never seen seafood shells so clean at the end of the meal! Not one scrap of flesh remains; it could take some conscientious diners as long as twenty minutes to dispatch a single crayfish!

Crayfish + snaps = kraftskiva

Recipe:

Crayfish party: the protocole
http://en.wikipedia.org/wiki/Crayfish_party

Restaurant | Famous Chef:

Sturehof, Stockholm
http://www.sturehof.com/

Assassin

You must be wondering how this chapter relates to the history of food. But I find this word's origin very interesting...

An assassin, of course, is someone who plans a murder for political ends. The word's etymology derives from the Arabic word *hashshashin* (an insulting term for the militant Shia Isma'ili sect who were followers of Hassan-i-Sabbah). Early targets included both Crusaders and Sunni Muslims. The word *hashshashin* itself comes from hashish; the paste made from the cannabis plant; meaning "to become dry" in Arabic.

Hashish is sometimes used as an ingredient in cookies and cakes: some readers might have encountered the so-called Space Cake. I have heard – second hand! – that this ingredient can completely transform a pedestrian *gateau au chocolat*. I have a friend – who prefers to remain anonymous – who has tried a little gustatory psychedelia. Though he insisted that he remained unaffected by his dessert, he did confess to me that he and his mates laughed rather more than usual that night.

Hashish, of course, is a forbidden substance; let no reader construe that I am endorsing it here!

Murder meets pleasure principle in one cake.

Recipe:

Space cake recipe
http://www.thestonerscookbook.com/recipe.php/recipe/space-cake

Baba

One of my favourite desserts is Paul Bocuse's variations of the classic *baba au rhum*. As a child, I loved this dessert because it was the only occasion when I was allowed rum: each baba was steeped in half a glass!

I like the round shape of the classical baba, the syrup's complex flavours derived from aged rum, and the crème pâtissière that fills its centre. I find the three contrasting textures – biscuit, liquid and airy cream – in perfect balance. I have only eaten two interpretations: Paul Bocuse's and my grandmother's. Please don't ask me to choose which I love better!

Baba (also given the affectionate diminutive 'babka') originated as sweetened bread made from rich dough baked in a steep cake tin. The first babkas were baked in the so-called Pale of Settlement, where the Russian, Austro-Hungarian and the Polish kingdoms met. In Polish and Russian, 'baba' means 'old woman' or 'granny': the cake was cylindrical and was baked in a fluted pan resembling a peasant woman's skirt.

Baba was introduced to France in the eighteenth century by Poland's exiled King Stanislas, who after he was deposed was appointed Duke of Lorraine. Having lost a kingdom, he acquired a cake. The royal pastry chef, Nicolas Stohrer, decided to soak dried baba in Malaga wine and add some crème pâtissière, perhaps in deference to local tastes.

Baba is closely related to the *kugelhopf* and the savarin, which uses the same dough in a ring mould, and kirsch rather than rum. The kugelhopf brings back memories of one of my chefs at the École Hotelière, one Jean-Louis Lichtenauer, who was from Alsace, and taught the preparation of meals for formal restaurants (technically referred to as "*le restaurant d'application*"). Perhaps due to his origins, the kugelhopf was Monsieur Lichtenauer's favourite dessert. It is baked in a deep circular mould with a central funnel; its sides are fluted with decorative swirls. The cake is then turned out and dusted with icing sugar, rather like fallen snow. In the old days, it was baked for Sunday breakfast, when the village baker would have his day of rest.

Recipe:

Baba recipe

http://ulteriorepicure.com/2009/12/25/edible-christmas-memory/

Restaurant | Famous Chef:

L'Aurberge du Pont de Collonges, Paul Bocuse, Lyons

http://www.bocuse.fr/accueil.aspx

Bain-Marie

We are all familiar with the bain-marie, which Americans know by the rather less romantic name double boiler. But I only recently learned the identity of the Marie who gave her name to the bath. Also known as Miriam, Marie was a historical figure who probably lived in Alexandria from the first to the third centuries BCE; she is sometimes confused with the Hebrew prophet Moses' sister, who was also called Miriam. An alchemist, the Alexandrian Miriam is sometimes credited with refining the chemical still, or three-armed distillation chamber.

When I was a child, Mamie and I would make *mousse au chocolat* together. She taught me how to melt chocolate in a small pan, balanced over water simmering beneath in a second, larger pan. Mamie showed me how her bain-marie raised the temperature gradually, so that the chocolate didn't burn, as it would if the heat were direct. As we all know, water boils at 100° F, so the bain-marie's maximum temperature is fixed just below boiling point of water.

Later, during my chef's apprenticeship, I learned other culinary applications for the bain-marie: when making cheesecake or custard, its use would prevent surfaces from unsightly cracks; or for Hollandaise and Béarnaise sauces, to prevent the egg yolk from curdling (which can happen at degrees about 63°). Pierre Gagnaire has created a 63 C° egg, in association with the chemist Hervé This: above that temperature, the texture of the yolk changes, and goes from liquid to something almost elastic. It becomes soft and malleable, like a paste.

In recent years, technology has evolved still further, and Joan Roca, chef at the prestigious Spanish restaurant El Celler de Can Roca, has created a new machine called the Roner, designed, as he says, to establish the precise "relationship between the ideal time and ideal temperature at which to cook fish and meat."

The Roner is a thermostat/ bain-marie that allows *sous-vide* cooking at a constant temperature (between 5° and 100°C). Food prepared at low temperatures is better able to preserve the molecular structure of proteins and amino acids without the flavours evaporating or colours dulling.

Before leaving Hong Kong, I organized a joint event between El Celler de Can Roca and the Mandarin Oriental's Grill + Bar. We were able to show Joan's brother and fellow Pastry chef Jordi that the Roner has become essential to our kitchens; in the Mandarin Grill alone five are in constant use.

Ave Maria!

Recipe:	**Restaurant	Famous Chef:**
Robuchon's mousse au chocolat recipe	*The Complete Robuchon,* pp. 722-23

Beaujolais Nouveau

Many readers will be familiar with Beaujolais Nouveau, but thanks to my origins as a son of Lyons, I hope to be able to give further insights. In Lyons, we joke that our city is crossed by three rivers: the Rhône, the Saône and the Beaujolais; it is our way of acknowledging the importance this wine has for our region. The heartland of Beaujolais' vineyards is just twenty minutes north of the city.

Beaujolais is a red wine made from the Gamay Noir a Jus Blanc grape; like the Champagne grape, each bunch must be picked by hand, since Beaujolais' wine making process requires that the cluster be whole. Its bouquet has accents of red fruit, banana and pear flavours. Beaujolais Nouveau is created through a process called carbonic maceration, or berry fermentation, which allows its consumption only a few weeks after the grapes are harvested. Carbonic maceration preserves the fresh, fruity quality of the wine without extracting bitter tannins from the grape skins.

There are ten growths, which at school I would reel off by heart, as if I were reciting a poem: Brouilly, Chenas, Chiroubles, Côtes de Brouilly, Fleurie, Juliénas, Morgon, Moulin-à-Vent, Régnié and the Valentine's Day favourite Saint-Amour. Beaujolais Nouveau, the first *primeur* wine, (*le vin de l'année*), is released at the end of the harvest, after 15 December.

But it is principally thanks to the marketing flair of *negociant* Georges Duboeuf that the Beaujolais Nouveau has achieved its current prominence. Duboeuf saw that selling young wine at a good profit would be a fine money spinner. He organized a race to Paris to bring the first bottles of the new vintage, which quickly evolved into a national event. Every year on the third Thursday in November, "Le Beaujolais Nouveau Est Arrivé" opens on the same day in more than 120 countries.

The creativity of Duboeuf does not stop there: he also had the concept of commissioning a different artist to design the label for each vintage. In 1993, he created Le Hameau du Vin, an amazing wine park, the first oenoparc ever, dedicated to the history of wines.

I had the chance to meet the man and his son, Franck, whilst organizing a school trip with my class from École Hotelière de Lausanne. I found them to be true visionaries in the field.

Restaurant | Famous Chef:

Le Café du Hameau restaurant, Georges Duboeuf, Romanèche-Thorins

http://www.hameauduvin.com/

BELLINI

A Bellini always reminds me of my first trip to Venice, which unfortunately was not in the company of a beautiful woman, but rather with my friend and then colleague, Luca de Mateo. No trip to the beautiful city known as Queen of the Adriatic is complete without a Bellini, which is a simple but perfect cocktail made of peach purée and Prosecco (Italian sparkling wine).

We owe its creation to a famous Italian called Giuseppe Cipriani (see also *Carpaccio*), who founded Harry's Bar. As a bartender in Venice's Hotel Europa, he was of course privy to the confidences of many of his customers. One regular, a wealthy young American, complained to him one day that his family had heard about his hard drinking and cut off his allowance. Giuseppe lent him money so he could go home to the United States; two years later the young man returned and repaid Giuseppe's kindness by giving him enough money to open a bar of his own. Giuseppe did just that, opening just off Venice's Piazza San Marco in 1931 and naming it Harry's after his patron.

Harry's Bar quickly became a Venice landmark, frequented by the likes of Ernest Hemingway and the European aristocracy, drawn there by the intimate atmosphere and Giuseppe's delicious peach and Prosecco invention. He named the cocktail after the Venetian painter Bellini, whose work can be seen all around the city, as the delicate pink hue of the drink resembled the colour of a saint's toga in one of his paintings.

The cocktail is now famous and a favourite worldwide, inspiring variations such as the Rossini, made with strawberry puree. Meanwhile from its humble beginnings, Harry's has expanded into a worldwide empire: Guiseppe's son Arrigo ('Harry' in Italian) and grandson Giuseppe now run Cipriani S.A, a large corporation owning luxury hotels, restaurants and clubs.

If you do not care for peach purée, you can always adapt the cocktail by substituting orange juice; you will have reinvented the drink as a Mimosa.

Salute!

Recipe:

Bellini recipe by Giana de Laurentiiis

http://www.foodnetwork.com/recipes/giada-de-laurentiis/bellini-bar-recipe/index.html

Restaurant | Famous Chef:

Harry's Bar, Venice

http://www.harrysbarvenezia.com/

Bibendum

The Michelin Man – whose nickname is Bibendum – is, as everybody knows, the trademark of the Michelin Company. It is one of the world's longest running logos. The Michelin guide, the world's oldest restaurant guide, was created in 1900 by André Michelin to help drivers choose places to eat and sleep while waiting for their cars to be repaired, and also to encourage them to wear out their tires in search of good food.

My first encounter with Bibendum was as a child, when I would visit my maternal grandfather at his Citroen garage near Lyons. The garage's walls were plastered with advertising from the Michelin tire company. Pape even gave me a key ring shaped like Bibendum.

I encountered the Man of Tires again when I lived in London, as I loved visiting Conran's South Kensington restaurant Bibendum – its food was so simple, so perfect, so creative. As a Frenchman, I was used to oysters being served reverently, on beautiful dishes, with flutes of Champagne; I loved how in contrast Bibendum chose to serve oysters from the back of a flatbed truck parked on the ground floor! And, larking around in the stained-glass windows, looking as cool and mischievous as he did when the Art Nouveau building was completed in 1909, was the man made of white tires himself.

My most recent encounter with Michelin was in Hong Kong, where

I met the Michelin guide Director at the time, Jean-Luc Naret, when he launched the first guide for Hong Kong and Macau in 2008. Naret was famous for his flamboyance – perhaps rather more than his predecessors were – but I found him charming; we share a passion for Provence and its regional cuisine. Learning that my parents lived in Provence, he recommended that I try Le Bistrot du Paradou; I found it an excellent tip, which I now pass on to you! But let's go back to Bibendum himself.

The Michelin brothers (André and Édouard) first commissioned the artist O'Galop to sketch Bibendum when Édouard got the idea after seeing a haphazard stack of bicycle tyres that resembled a fat man. The name itself was borrowed from a verse of the Roman poet Horace: *Nunc est Bibendum,* meaning 'Time to drink!' Rossillon's original sketch showed Bibendum toasting the viewer with a glass full of road hazards like nails and broken glass ('Michelin tyres drink up roadblocks!'). His rivals, punctured and leaking air, look enviously on.

How strange that a chef's most sought-after accolade should have originated as a marketing ploy to sell tires!

Recipe: **Restaurant | Famous Chef:**

Simon Hopkinson's Fish & Chips   *The Bibendum Cookbook*, 48-51

BIG APPLE

I consider myself fortunate for having visited 32 countries and lived in eleven (and counting!). When asked which country I prefer most, my answer is always, each one. Everywhere I live, I learn something new; I leave richer in knowledge of different cultures, religions and – of course! – cuisines.

We often judge the habitants of a country according to what and how they eat. I am sure you are familiar with the expression Frogs (the sometimes rude, sometimes affectionate name that the British have for the French) and *les Rosbifs* ('the Roast beefs' the French counter nickname for the British, which owes something to their love of cattle and something to their often florid complexions)! During my travels I am frequently amused at the unusual nicknames that many of the world's major cities have.

The Big Apple is one of the most famous; have you ever wondered why we call New York the Big Apple?

The story is actually very simple and is unrelated to any apple trees in Central Park. A journalist called John Fitz Gerald referred to the Big Apple while writing about horse racing for the New York *Morning Telegraph*. The first reference was in 1924, when Fitz Gerald wrote:

> *The Big Apple. The dream of every lad that ever threw a leg over a thoroughbred and the goal of all horsemen. There's only one Big Apple. That's New York.*

The expression caught on among other journalists and, after a calculated ad campaign in the 1970s, actually became city's second name.

But New York is not the only city around the world with a nickname: Paris is known as the City of Lights. I've also lived in Bangkok ("Venice of the East"), Stockholm ("Venice of the North"), London ("The Big Smoke"), Hong Kong ("The Big Lychee") …

Recipe:

Apple pie recipe from Pastis

http://www.pastisny.com/

BISCUIT | AFTERNOON TEA

As a child after school, I would often stay with my grandmother. She would serve me *goûter*, or *quatre-heures* – a reference to the time the meal was served (four o'clock in the afternoon), or Afternoon Tea in England. In France, we normally have coffee, tea or a *chocolat chaud* with *tartines*, or biscuits. The biscuit must be a hard and crispy wafer that we dip into our drinks so it will be soft when we eat it. Mamie served a perfectly done *chocolat chaud* with *tartines*, which she made from delicious bread that was left over from lunch.

Paul Jackson, my predecessor at the Mandarin Oriental Hong Kong, today's General Manager at Claridge's, wrote this elegant account of the origin of High Tea: "It was the seventh duchess of Bedford, Anna Maria Russell, who in 1840 decided that eight hours was more than one woman should be expected to wait for dinner. She therefore instructed her butler to bring tea, bread and butter to her drawing room at five o'clock. She then began inviting friends to join her to discuss latest fashions and scandals, and a new institution was born. The Aerated Bread Company founded the first tearoom almost twenty years later, but the most famous of all was opened by J. Lyons in Piccadilly, London in 1894."

After I graduated from L'École Hotelière de Lausanne, my first job was as the head of food and beverage at Edinburgh's Balmoral Hotel. We served the best afternoon tea in Scotland at our glamorous Palm Court, which is justly famous for its circular room underneath a glittering glass canopied dome. We would serve the classic three stepped plates, with finger sandwiches, *choux* tartlets, and – of course! – scones with clotted cream.

The word *biscuit* comes from the medieval French word *bis-cuit*, ("cooked twice"), and is related to the Italian *biscotto*, and the Dutch *beschuit*. Biscuits originated as a foodstuff for sailors, who would carry flour, water and eggs on their ships; they cooked their dough twice to preserve it from spoiling.

Whatever you're doing at four o'clock, drop it for tea!

Recipe:	**Restaurant	Famous Chef:**
Scottish shortbread	*The Leith Cookery Bible*, 626

Bloody Mary

Have you ever thought about the name of this famous cocktail? Who was Mary, anyway? And why was she bloody?

For me, the Bloody Mary is synonymous with brunch. When I opened Café Oliver in Madrid in 2002, we served the first ever brunch in town, offering all types of eggs, *viennoiserie*, salads and cocktails like the Bellini, Mimosa and Bloody Mary. I used to sell a huge number of Bloody Marys by claiming that it was the best drink to cure a hangover: hair of the dog that bit you, as the Irish say (or *de quoi reprendre du poil de la bête,* as we French say!). My nutritionist friend always retorts that the drink's celery is excellent for the kidneys, and the tomato is full of vitamin C, and *that's* what cures the hangover. We agree to differ...

The original "Bloody Mary" was England's Mary Tudor, who earned herself the sobriquet after executing several hundred Protestants, all in a futile effort to reverse her father Henry VIII's break with the Roman Catholic Church. Some 400 years later Fernand Petiot, the Parisian bartender at Harry's New York Bar, created the cocktail in 1920. In an interview before his death, Petiot claimed that he invented it according to the specifications of two Chicago patrons, who told him that back home they drank a version called "Bucket of Blood" served by a waitress everyone knew as Bloody Mary. Petiot himself improved on the drink's vodka and tomato juice base by adding salt, lemon juice and Tabasco hot sauce.

There are countless variations; some popular ones are the Dickson's

Bloody Mary, which also contains sherry and horseradish, the Bloody Maria, made with tequila, and the Caesar – not for the faint-hearted – with its base of Clamato, or a mixture of tomato juice and clam broth.

At Hong Kong's Mandarin Oriental, we would serve about twenty variations on the Bloody Mary: Bloody Geishas (with sake); Bloody Fairies (absinthe); Bloody Marias (tequila)…

Personally, the versions I like best are the Virgin Mary (without alcohol) and the Bull Shot, which substitutes beef consommé for the tomato juice. On Sunday you can find me at Electric House with Simon McCabe, the "mayor of Notting Hill", on Portobello Road sipping a Bloody Mary with celery stalk and green olives.

Thirsty?

Recipe:

Fernand Petiot traditional recipe

http://www.cocktailtimes.com/vodka/bloodymary.shtml

Bocuse d'Or

The Bocuse d'Or is a biannual contest held in my hometown, Lyons. Commonly known as the culinary Oscars, the Bocuse d'Or might be more fittingly compared with the Olympics, such are its demands for stamina, training, and skill. Over two days, the competition gives 24 chefs from different countries only 5½ hours to create both a fish platter and a meat platter, all while fans are screaming wildly in the stands: the noise makes concentration very difficult. The Bocuse d'Or Committee specifies (and provides) the fish and meat, while the contestants select their own accompaniments and garnishes. A panel of the cooking world's best and brightest first judge a platter's look; then they taste. "You live and die in eight bites," said one chef.

Founded in 1987, the contest is named after Monsieur Paul, who "conceived the Bocuse d'Or as a competition in which young chefs from around the world would come to Lyons and cook the food of their homelands for a panel of judges." Interviewed by Andrew Friedman for *Knives at Dawn*, an account of the US team's experience in 2007-08, Bocuse says the prize was conceived in reaction to the lacklustre global cooking of the 1970s and 1980s: "It was the time of broccoli, kiwi, and avocados!"

Contestants are chosen after regional knock-out competitions: Bocuse d'Or Europe, Bocuse d'Or Asia, and the Copa Azteca in Mexico City. At the finals in Lyons, taste accounts for forty of sixty possible points, with the platters' presentation earning the rest. If there is a tie, then 'kitchen management' points are allowed to designate a winner.

Each contestant used to cook in a little 3m'6m Enodis kitchen 'pod,' fitted with a combi oven, an industrial strength salamander, blast chiller, and an electric range. Great precision is demanded of the chefs who compete, even down to the limits on platter sizes, which must be no larger than 43" by 27". As the competition has evolved, dishes have become ever more complex and virtuoso, yet each chef must make everything from scratch on the day, barring certain items like stock and puff pastries, which may be brought in.

What is the Bocuse d'Or's value? Training for the competition is the equivalent of more than ten years' experience in a kitchen. As Roland Henin, Thomas Keller's mentor and ex-coach for the Bocuse d'Or American team, says: "The Bocuse d'Or is not what you cooked five or ten years ago. It's what you're cooking today, for the judge. It's not where you've been. It's not who you know. It's what you do under those circumstances… You push yourself to the point that you didn't know that you were able to push or achieve."

Recipe:

Winning recipe from Geir Skeie's cookbook

Restaurant | Famous Chef:

World Champion from Childhood to the Bocuse d'O

BOUCHON

A bouchon is a restaurant unique to Lyons; it serves regional specialties like *tablier de sapeur* (breaded tripe), *quenelle de brochet* (pike quenelles) in crayfish butter bechamel (sauce Nantua), and *cervelle de Canut* (fromage blanc with olive oil, shallots, and chopped herbs). Each bouchon has a traditional atmosphere, and many have tiled walls and marble topped tables. Though similar to the bistro, a bouchon is more casual and rather better value for money.

No one quite knows where the name *bouchon* comes from: the plait of straw – similar to a bottle stopper – that signified a restaurant during the late medieval age ('bousche' in Old French); the cork (*bouchon de paille*) shaped straw used to rub down visitors' horses; the straw strewn across the floor of the restaurants to stop patrons from slipping. Though more than 200 restaurants that claim the title 'bouchon,' only twenty-one belong to the Authentic Bouchon Association. To belong, a restaurant must fit certain criteria; the first being that the establishment may not even own a freezer! Association members display a picture of Gnafron, our Lyonnais puppet equivalent of England's Punch. His nose is red from drinking too much!

Bouchons always serve a Beaujolais or a Côte du Rhône (the wine regions nearest my hometown) served in a thick glass carafe (the famous *pot Lyonnais*, which at 46 centilitres is about half the size of an ordinary wine bottle). Different colour bands on the pot's neck signals the wine's identity. The pot Lyonnais are designed to be stable, as drinkers will leave them on gravel during a game of *boule Lyonnaise*.

My favourite bouchon is Le Mercière, which is run by Louis Manoa, whom we all call Le Viking, because he's got blond hair and he can be (good-naturedly) rough. Le Mercière is one of the oldest bouchons in Lyon and is still famous from the part it played helping Resistance fighters and Jews escape capture during WW2. A little *traboule,* or covered alley, cuts the bouchon in two; built so that the city's famous silks could be moved between ateliers during bad weather, the *traboules* helped fugitives evade their Nazi pursuers. Though its heroic days are over, Le Mercière is still amazing: it has the smallest kitchen I have ever seen, just 3-4 m². Yet somehow, they can handle up to 200 covers when the pavement tables are full! And the food is wonderful: I especially love the pike quenelles with sauce Nantua.

Another favourite bouchon of mine is Abel; a great restaurant – to go to the toilet, you have to go through the kitchen. You can see the chef shouting at his staff, urging them on; you can feel the stress at work. Murmuring, 'Sorry! Sorry!' you squeeze past the kitchen staff. Abel is a beautiful place, with different floor levels, ceramic tiles, mirrors with the menus written out in white pen; the dish of the day displayed on a chalkboard.

As Gnafron would say, "At work we can only do our best, but when eating, we should spare no effort!"

Recipe:

Tablier de Sapeur recipe

http://www.theworldwidegourmet.com/recipes/breaded-tripe-tablier-de-sapeur/

Restaurant | Famous Chef:

Le Mercière, Louis Manoa, Lyons

http://www.le-merciere.fr/

Bouillabaisse

Anyone who has visited Marseille on France's Riviera should have eaten bouillabaisse at least once: the restaurant Miramar claims to serve the authentic version, although it has many rivals vying for that title.

Classical bouillabaisse is a fish soup made with only Mediterranean fish, some vegetables and spices. The name bouillabaisse comes from the Occitan, *bolhabaissa*, which describes the cooking method of boiling the broth (*bolhir*) and then adding the fishes one by one, reducing the temperature to a simmer (*abaissar*).

As with so many classic dishes, bouillabaisse has very humble origins. At the end of each day, Marseille fishermen would cook on the pier and eat the remaining fish – either those that were difficult to sell, like the ones with too many bones, or those that were very ugly, like the hideous but delicious *racasse*. The fishermen would then boil them in water with garlic and fennel and the broth would reduce to a soup consistency. Later variations included tomato and, as the dish became a specialty in local restaurants, more luxurious ingredients such as saffron were added. Pierre Gagnaire makes a special version, served cold with the stock converted into jelly and the cooked fish morsels placed on top.

Bouillabaisse is so popular and has undergone so many transformations as it has been reinterpreted around the world, that in 1980 a group of restaurants in Marseille and around France reacted by forming a charter (La Charte de la Bouillabaisse Marseillaise) to 'protect' the original recipe. La Charte specifies the correct ingredients: conger, scorpion fish, weaver, monkfish, sea robin, tomato, potato, onion, garlic, saffron, cumin, fennel, olive oil, parsley, salt, and pepper. It suggests serving the broth separately from the fish, in deference to the traditional Marseillaise fashion. Finally, La Charte members insist that bouillabaisse must be served with *rouille* sauce, a kind of mayonnaise mixed with saffron, garlic and cayenne pepper and with thin toasted slices of baguette.

And I insist that white wine from Bandol or Châteauneuf du Pape accompany the dish!

Recipe:

The Miramar recipe from JP Coffe

http://www.jeanpierrecoffe.com/recette/266-la-bouillabaisse-du-miramar

Restaurant | Famous Chef:

Restaurant Miramar, Marseille

http://www.bouillabaisse.com/cadre.php

Boxing Day

It was during my time in Edinburgh that I first learned about Boxing Day. Once I could understand the Scots dialect (no easy feat for me), I began to learn the local customs. I could not understand why 26 December was a public holiday, and why Christmas festivities continued on that day, with everyone eating Very Rich Fruitcakes and leftovers.

Boxing Day is mainly celebrated throughout the Commonwealth of Nations. There are many foundation myths surrounding Boxing Day, but it seems to have evolved principally as a day for giving in money, gifts or leftover food to society's neediest.

During the Age of Exploration, a priest would bring a small container (known as 'the Christmas Box'), onto the sailing ships while they were anchored at port; the act was thought to bring luck. The crewmen themselves would drop money into the box to pray for the ship's safe return. The box was then sealed and handed back to the priest if the ship returned safe, in thanks for his having offered prayers. The priest would wait for Christmas to open the box, and then share the money among the parish's poor.

During the Victorian era, it was common for tradesmen to collect their Christmas boxes, made of wood or clay, from neighbouring aristocrats in exchange for services rendered during the year. This tradition still exists with porters, cleaners, and receptionists, or even – despite these recession-hit times – the Christmas bonus among some companies.

For the servants of the landowners, Boxing Day was also the day they would visit their families, picking up bonuses and leftover food. Once again, the customs from the past explains our current behaviour, as 26 December is also the first day of the Sales in many countries and one of the biggest sales days of the year.

Don't forget to give!

Recipe:

Very Rich Fruit Cake

Restaurant | Famous Chef:

The Art of Home Cooking, 135-8

BRUNCH

It must be obvious to all that the word 'brunch' comes from a combination of 'breakfast' and 'lunch.' Brunch usually is served from 11AM to 3PM, and starts with a hot drink, freshly squeezed juice, *viennoiserie* (*pains au chocolat, pains aux raisins,* brioche, *pains au lait,* croissants) and eggs; brunch may also include salads and carved meat, before closing with a dessert.

When I co-owned Café Oliver in Madrid, we were the first to introduce brunch to Spain. It was 2002, and very much an alien concept, one rooted in the Anglo-Saxon world, where week-end breakfasts could run so late that they ran into lunch. Café Oliver would serve a mix of traditional dishes from America and Britain – omelettes and eggs Benedict, for instance.

At first, the Spanish disparaged the meal as *broonch*, and our customers were all foreigners. Then we began to have artists and actresses: Penelope Cruz and Javier Bardem. Then Madrid embraced us: Café Oliver was even immortalized by Spain's Carrie Bradshaw, Mariana Jara, in her book *Kisses with a Taste of Kir Royal*: *Toni hace dias que andaba esquivo, complicado y taciturno. Las cosas no le van muy bien y no es porque haya llegado sin afeitar a nuestro brunch del Cafe Oliver...*

"Toni has been looking reserved, strange and stubborn lately. Things are not going very well for him, and it is not because he arrived at our brunch at Café Oliver without shaving..."

Now there are many places in Madrid that serve brunch, but we were the first.

For me, brunch is synonymous with meeting friends and catching up on things that have happened since we last met. When living in Paris, I liked to try a different brunch spot every Sunday. I quite liked Pain Quotidien, Belgium concept and chain, based on a communal table with the pots of jams open in the table's centre; I also liked the bakery, where I would buy *viennoiserie* to take away.

The most memorable brunch I have eaten (to date!) was served the day after my wedding, which lasted a marathon three days. We organized it in my parents' house in Provence. My mother had the village's pizza truck parked in the middle of our family's garden. The *pizzaiolo* made a beautiful thin crust pizza with toppings that the guests chose; the pizza was accompanied with reds or rosés from the Domaine de Valdition, our local *vin de pays des Alpilles*.

Looking forward to next Sunday – as always.

Recipe:

Brunch Menu from Café Oliver

http://cafeoliver.com/comer-en-cafe-oliver/el-brunch/

Restaurant | Famous Chef:

Café Oliver, Madrid

www.cafeoliver.com

Bûche de Noël

In the many years that I have lived abroad, I try to return to my family for Christmas. That season is always a chance to go over what has happened in the preceding year, and to eat la Bûche de Noël, also called the Yule log.

In its classic incarnation, la Bûche is a sponge cake made with flour, sugar, eggs and chocolate. It resembles a log decorated with marzipan trees, a snowman, mushrooms, or even axes. No one in my family makes it – it's so much work! – so we would buy ours from Delhomme (a patisserie justly famous for its delicious opera cakes and *tarte aux pralines* dusted with red sugar). Modern versions may crunch or have ice-cream on the inside. My own preferred Yule log has chestnuts.

American readers should note that in France it is unusual to buy cakes where you buy bread, as the specialties are considered very different. With patisserie, you are dealing with eggs, fruits, and sugar; with croissants and baguettes, with dough.

La Bûche has pagan roots: in pre-Roman Gaul during the winter solstice, a huge log that consumed itself slowly (either beech, elm, oak, or cherry would do) was set alight in a symbolic effort to bank and rekindle the vanishing sun's fire. Ideally the log would last Twelve Days of Christmas: from 25 December to 6 January, Epiphany on the Christian calendar.

A fruit tree's wood supposedly guaranteed a good crop for the following year, and the log would normally be blessed with a box branch and laurel kept from Easter Sunday. In some regions, wine was poured to ensure a good vintage; in others, salt was thrown in to scare away witches.

Even if you have no chimney, you can still enjoy la Bûche: in the States, a burning log appears on flat screen TVs: a Neolithic tradition goes high-tech.

Restaurant | Famous Chef:

Patisserie Delhomme, Lyons

http://www.achat-lyon.com/ann2219-PATISSERIE-DELHOMME.htm

Cacao Beans

Who is not fond of chocolate? Everyone loves it! Yet when first introduced to Europe it was frowned on as an aphrodisiac and an effeminate beverage; in pre-Columbian Mexico, by contrast, it was a drink for Aztec warriors, who brought ground cacao as rations when on their campaigns. An ironic origin for the stuff of Valentines.

Whenever I eat chocolate, I remember being a child, when I would buy myself a bar of dark chocolate to eat with a piece of crusty baguette for *goûter* or *quatre-heures*, as we called it; a Gallic reinterpretation of England's Afternoon Tea. I would even eat that chocolate sandwich as my school lunch in second grade; it was the best way to use the ten francs my parents gave me each day. The cost of the bar chocolate and half baguette was around 2 FF, which meant that I still had 8 FF to play baby foot (table football) with my friends. We got four games in, and my parents were none the wiser.

Chocolate is made from cacao beans, fruit of the evergreen cacao tree. Its cultivated origins are ancient: it was first domesticated by the Central American Olmec peoples around 1400 BC. The beans were even used as currency throughout Central America. The English word chocolate perhaps derives from the Aztec Nahuatl word *chicolatl* ('beaten water'), though it may also come from the word *xocoatl*, which referred to the unsweetened drink made from cocoa beans and other seasonings like vanilla.

The Spanish conquistadores brought chocolate – which they knew as 'black almonds' – to European courts. Though marketed for its medicinal qualities, chocolate quickly became associated with louche practices: by the seventeenth century, Madame du Barry, mistress of Louis XV, supposedly relied on it to help the king get an erection. The Marquis de Sade was sentenced to death after being accused of abusing chocolate during an infamous orgy, where he mixed it with Spanish fly (cantharides), a pre-modern Viagra that could poison if the dosage were miscalculated.

Scientists, however, deny that chocolate has aphrodisiac qualities. Though it does contain some cannabinoid chemicals similar to the active ingredient in marijuana, and some phenylethylamine, a naturally occurring body chemical that has amphetamine-like effects, these amounts are too slight to cause addiction; according to Harold McGee (*The Science and Lore of the Kitchen):* it is the sensory experience of eating chocolate alone, "no more and no less, that is powerfully appealing."

Need a cup?

Restaurant | Famous Chef:

Patrick Roger, Paris

http://www.patrickroger.com/site/en/index.htm

CAESAR SALAD

Where does the Caesar Salad get its name? From the Emperor Caesar Augustus? Maybe from the Caesar Palace in Las Vegas? You might be surprised to learn that the answer is 'no' on both counts.

This classic salad was invented over a Fourth of July weekend by Caesar Cardini, who ran the Hotel Commercial in Tijuana, Mexico. The first Caesar Salad included Romaine lettuce, croutons, lemon juice, olive oil, egg, Worcestershire sauce and black pepper. It had no chicken or anchovies, which were added to the recipe only later by the creator's brother Alex.

Caesar's daughter Rosa says that her father invented the salad by happy accident: his kitchen was almost empty, so he threw together all the ingredients he had with condiments from the dressing table.

Every single restaurant where I have ever worked has served this salad; each chef puts his own signature on it, whether by the method of slicing, the meat's temperature, or how it's served. The simplicity of Café Oliver's version makes it my favourite: Romaine lettuce, croutons made from French baguette pan-fried in olive oil to give them a lovely yellow green colour, Parmeggiano Reggiano shavings, anchovies only faintly salty, and pan fried chicken breast cut into strips. The dressing was made of Spanish virgin olive oil, wine vinegar, egg yolk, black pepper, crushed garlic and anchovies. Don't add any salt, as the anchovies provide more than enough. The main difference with the American version is the addition of anchovies within the dressing and on the salad.

Caesar Salad

At Hong Kong's Mandarin Oriental, we would serve a Caesar salad in miniature as canapés. The parmesan would be slightly melted and then shaped into a purse that would be filled with chopped Romaine lettuce, anchovies, croutons and dressing.

When I think of Caesar salads, I remember Sunday brunches in Madrid and Café Oliver's beautiful sash windows open to the winds; the city's international crowd would gather and catch up on the previous night's gossip. Spain's new generation of actors would come in: Leonor Watling, Javier Camara, (both actors who appeared in Pedro Almodovar's beautiful movie *Talk to Her)*, Penelope Cruz' sister Monica…

Can't wait till next Sunday!

Recipe:

Caesar Cardini original recipe

http://www.kitchenproject.com/history/CaesarSalad/OriginalRecipeCaesarSalad.htm

Restaurant | Famous Chef:

Dean & Deluca Cookbook, page 16

CARAT

What does the word *carat* have to do with the history of food? More than you might think!

My family were jewellers in Lyons for 150 years, specializing in filigree. My great-great-grandfather, Jean-Francois Melon, founded the company in 1850. According to family tradition, I should have taken over the business; but once I had eaten at Paul Bocuse's restaurant, I knew that I wanted a life centred around food. But although I chose a different path, my father, Pierre Melon, continued to educate me about jewellery and precious stones. In this entry, my father's world and the world I chose for myself, overlap.

Since the nineteenth century, the carat has been used to measure weight for the four precious stones – diamonds, rubies, emeralds and sapphires – as well as pearls.

Still fail to see the link between jewels and food? Under the Byzantine Empire, merchants would use a vegetable seed renowned for its uniform weight (20mg). The fruit is called the *carob*, which belongs to the pea tree family and grows wild in the eastern Mediterranean. The word comes from the Greek *keration*, meaning 'carob seed.'

So, a 10 carats diamond weighs as much as 10 carob seeds: 20g. Their values, of course, are unfortunately somewhat different…

But the word carat can also be written with a "k" (in American English); this *karat* refers to the gold's purity. (I am sure that my readers must be familiar with the expression '24-karat gold'!) The karat corresponds to 1/24 of mass purity. Therefore 24-karat is 100% gold, whereas 18-karat is 75% and 12 karat 50%...

Nowadays each region of the world has its preference. In Hong Kong and China, customers prefer 24-karat, locally known as *Chuk Kam*, while in India 22-karat is preferred; in Europe and the US, 18-karat is standard. The lesser the gold content, the more malleable the metal is.

That should explain why my father decided to work with ten carat stones, while I offer ten carob seeds as bar snacks for my customers!

Carbonara

As I was married to an Italian wife from Rome, I was forced to understand Italian cuisine, which is the source of all European cuisine... please agree and don't argue!

I think that the spaghetti carbonara must be one of the most popular and famous pasta dishes in the world – no five star hotel's room service menu is complete without it – and though I have often eaten carbonara at home, I never wondered about its provenance until I began this book.

The word *carbonara* relates to charcoal, which has given rise to explanations claiming that the term referred to Italian charcoal workers who perhaps would cook the dish over a grill. The name carbonara may also recall Rome's charcoal makers, the Carbonari, a nineteenth century secret society made up primarily of intellectuals and others who sought the unification of Italy. Celebrated members included Lord Byron and Louis Napoleon Bonaparte.

But most historians think that the carbonara is a relatively recent invention, a dish concocted to use up surplus eggs, cream, and bacon that the American army brought as surplus rations after entering the Eternal City in June 1944. If this is perhaps a cynical creation story for this well-loved dish, it is also true that whatever carbonara's origins, the Romans have made it their own. Carbonara went international after American GI's brought the recipe home after WW2.

I recommend using spaghetti rather than rigatoni, pecorino Romano (rather than Parmiggiano), *guanciale,* which is cured fatty pork, and a heavy cream.

I like the creaminess of a perfect carbonara. You have to add the cooked pasta to the raw egg yolk so the pasta's heat will coagulate the eggs. Remember that egg yolks start coagulating above 63°C, so you must wait a few minutes once you have drained the pasta. It is probably the only pasta recipe I do not recommend adding salt in the water, as the saltiness will come from the bacon.

In Lausanne, my flatmate Fabrice Gavaret and I made this our signature dish – perhaps because the carbohydrates are recommended to cure hangovers.

A tavola!

Recipe:	**Restaurant	Famous Chef:**
Carbonara recipe from my father-in-law Roberto della Rovere	Restaurant Vivaldi, Roquetas del Mar
	http://www.paginasamarillas.es/fichas/ig/vivaldi-restaurante_197952500_000000001.html

Carnival

My first memories of Carnival were televised images of Rio of Janeiro, or, closer to home, Nice's Carnival along the Cote d'Azur. But I first participated in a carnival in London's Notting Hill. Organized in 1959 to celebrate the Caribbean heritage of London's immigrant communities, the Notting Hill Carnival has now become the world's second largest street festival. From Portobello Road to Westbourne Grove where I now live, the streets are packed with people from across the globe, while stands offer drinks and snacks as dancers in glowing skimpy dresses circulate throughout the streets and Caribbean music blares from the trucks and buses decked out the occasion.

Carnival is celebrated just before Lent, the Christian calendar's forty day fast that commemorates Jesus' time in the desert when he was tempted by Satan. Lent ends with Easter, which celebrates Jesus' resurrection.

Carne vale is a late Latin phrase that means *Good-bye to meat,* as during the next 40 days (known as *Car-ême* in French) Christians are supposed to avoid rich, luxurious food. The peak of the Carnival is Mardi Gras, which is also known as Fat Tuesday; the last three days of Carnival end on the Tuesday before Ash Wednesday, when Lent begins.

In today's secular world, we live far removed from the origins for our traditions; few know the origins of celebrations like Shrove Tuesday, when pancakes are traditionally served. For that holiday, Mamie always served delicious *matefaim* ('cut the hunger'), which were savoury pancakes (topped with fried eggs, ham, or cheese) followed by sweet ones (lemon with sugar, or a *confiture* jam).

'Rich' ingredients – eggs, milk, and sugar – must be consumed before the Lenten fast begins. Pancakes and doughnuts were an efficient way of using up these perishable goods, and psychologically they also provided a time of release and abandon and pleasure, before the introspection and austerity of Lent began.

So, the next time you join a carnival, whilst you are watching the beautiful sinuous dancers, try and remember that the festivities have religious roots, and that you are celebrating the last days of meat before fasting begins.

Happy Meat…

Recipe:

Matefaim recipe

http://www.yummytime.com/recipe/995/MATEFAIM-LYONNAIS

Carpaccio

I love to eat Carpaccio on hot days when I want something light and fresh: a Carpaccio with rocket salad on the side is perfect. The cut of beef is extremely important: I prefer to eat only the tenderloin.

Giuseppe Cipriani, founder of the Harry's Bar in Venice (*see Bellini*) first invented the Carpaccio. One day Countess Amalia Nani Mocenigo came for lunch and explained that she had a special diet: her doctor had ordered her to eat only raw meat. The Carpaccio, made of thin slices of raw beef topped with olive oil and parmesan, was created for her.

The name Carpaccio comes from the famous Venetian painter Vittore Carpaccio. Cipriani, who loved the painter's work, named the dish after him: the raw beef's red reminded him of the tint used in *The Legend of Saint Ursula*, a series of nine paintings.

These days the word Carpaccio refers to any meat, fish or even fruit cut raw in thin slices. Uwe Opocensky, ex Hong Kong's Mandarin Oriental Executive Chef, prepared a Carpaccio which looks like the original one, but is made from watermelon. Uwe worked for Ferran Adrià at El Bulli, and like his mentor, comes up with crazy wonderful ideas. For his Carpaccio, Uwe slices watermelon into thin, almost translucent slices; vacuum packs them to dry them out; then he poaches them in a bag, and though it *looks* like a thin slice of meat, the texture has completely changed. It's become a meat texture. Uwe custom made a rack – he hangs the watermelon as if it was meat drying. Then he adds honey and nuts. When he would serve it in the summer, he would bring each dish to the Krug Room (the

Mandarin's chef's table), and he would say to customers, "I'll let you try this, and then discover what it is for yourself." People would guess wildly. "Is it meat? Tomato? Red pepper?" Sometimes I thought it looked like something a cannibal would want to gnaw on. Out of 100 people, only about two knew what their Carpaccio really was: that says a lot about how much the eye tells you about what you're having.

To make Carpaccio at home, freeze your tenderloin and then slice it on a machine to get the requisite thin slices (3mm width). Then add salt and pepper, virgin olive oil, and parmesan shavings; scatter some rocket leaves and drizzle lemon dressing on top.

Buon appetito!

Recipe:

Harry's Bar Carpaccio recipe

http://www.justfoodnow.com/2010/01/25/harrys-bar-carpaccio/

Restaurant | Famous Chef:

Harry's Bar, Venice

http://www.cipriani.com/locations/venice/restaurants/harrys-bar.php

Catty & Tael

Those readers who have lived or travelled in Asia have surely heard these words, either at a restaurant or when buying food at a wet market.

'Catty' is an English word borrowed from the Malay (*kati*); it refers to the Chinese unit of measurement used throughout Southeast Asia. Confusingly, however, there is no universally agreed value for the catty: each country assigns its own. In Hong Kong one catty equals 604.78g. Other countries – like Taiwan and Thailand – have rounded the figure down to 600g, while China rounded down even further to 500g. The lack of standardization between figures reflects each country's colonial and mercantile histories.

Tael comes from the Malay *tahi*, meaning 'weight.' One tael equals roughly 40g, or 1/16 of a catty.

Candareen	1/1600
Mace	1/160
Tael	1/16
Catty	1
Picul	100

You will greatly impress restaurant staff, should you be able to order live fish in a Chinese restaurant using this system.

My recommendation for two persons, a 2 catties fish!

Club des Chefs des Chefs

I came across the Club des Chefs des Chefs (the CCC) in 2009 thanks to "*mon ami*" Cassam Gooljarry, now deceased, the oldest French resident in Hong Kong. He knows everybody who is anybody and introduced me to Gilles Bragard.

Gilles Bragard and his wife Monica are known as the couturiers of chefware. The Bragard Company, founded in 1933 in the Vosges by Gilles' father, makes the world's finest hospitality uniforms. With Paul Bocuse, Bragard created a vest, called "Grand Chef," which is worn by the best chefs worldwide. The celebrity chef Joël Robuchon once complained that the vests then available on the market all had uncomfortable collars: Bragard designers were happy to adapt the cut to Robuchon's specifications.

In 1977 Gilles Bragard founded one of the most exclusive clubs in the world, called the Club des Chefs des Chefs, when he brought together the chefs to the President of the United States and to the President of France over a meal at Paul Bocuse's restaurant, Collonges au Mont d'Or. Now its 30-odd members include chefs to heads of state and monarchs from around the world, including France, Britain, the United States, China and India. The club meets every year in a different country; I was proud to host their visit in August 2010 at the Mandarin Oriental in Hong Kong, when I was made an honorary CCC member. The club's itinerary included a visit to the restaurant Forum, whose chef Ah Yat is famous as the city's 'King of Abalone,' and to the Mandarin's Connaught Rooms, where Chef

Uwe Opocensky reinterpreted classic Chinese dim sum dishes, creating a unique tea (made of chives, gold leaf, and edible flowers), whose gelatine bag dissolved after a consommé was poured into the cup; his mango custards and sweet dim sum desserts arrived in tiny birdcages.

Valued for their discretion as much as their culinary expertise, the annual CCC meeting is a chance for the state chefs to relax and discuss the unique responsibilities that come with cooking everything from elaborate state banquets to light family suppers for world leaders. Knowing that historic decisions are made over their creations brings intense pressure to the job, but as Bragard sums up with the club's motto: "Politics divides men, but a good meal unites them."

And of course, M. Bragard, who has attended every meeting of the club since 1977, has ensured that the Chefs des Chefs have their own special 'Grand Chef', embroidered with their countries' flags and seals. Once asked which cuisine in the world was the best, Bragard responded with customary diplomacy: "In this club, we each say, 'Our mother's."

So now you know the identity of chef ware's Christian Dior, and which Club is the most exclusive in the world! Don't forget to wear your "Grand Chef"!

Recipe:

Uwe's gold-flecked tea recipe

Restaurants | Famous Chefs:

Club des Chefs des Chefs

http://www.webspawner.com/users/lechefsofstate/clubdesches.html

Bragard USA

http://www.bragardusa.com/

Châteauneuf Du Pape

I have always had a preference for the wines from the Rhône region: they are so underrated, I feel, when compared with the more celebrated (but also considerably more expensive) Burgundy and Bordeaux wines.

Châteauneuf-du-Pape is the most famous appellation from the southern Rhône valley, just north of Avignon. Avignon was the capital of Catholicism for over 70 years during the fourteenth century. Pope Clement V – the same pope who ordered the arrest of the Knights Templar on Friday, 13 October 1307, hence Friday the thirteenth being considered an unlucky day – ordered the planting of vines, though he was never to drink the wine: it was his successor John XXII who actually founded the vineyards, creating the first *vin du Pape*. John XXII also founded the palatial retreat that would give the appellation its own name: "Châteauneuf-du-Pape," or "Pope's New Castle."

Rules drawn up in 1923 allow thirteen vine varieties to go into Châteauneuf-du-Pape. Here is the list: Grenache and Cinsault for sweetness, warmth and mellowness. Mourvèdre, Syrah, Muscardin and Camarèse for robustness, maturity, colour and a thirst-quenching taste. Counoise and Picpoul for charm and a special bouquet. (The poet Frédéric Mistral claimed that the Counoise variety was a gift from Spain to Pope Urbain V.) Clairette and Bourboulenc for finesse, fire and brilliance. But also, Terret Noir and Vaccarèse (both red grapes), and Picardin and Roussane, which are white.

One of the characteristics of Châteauneuf-du-Pape is that its terroir often has *galets roulés*, "rolling stones" (see *Rolling Stone*) scattered throughout the clay soil. These stones absorb the sun's heat; at night, they release this warmth, which helps the grapes to ripen faster.

I myself especially love white Châteauneuf-du-Pape, with its flavours that range from mineral to oily, and its hints of almond, fennel and even star fruit. I recommend Château de Beaucastel, Perrin & Fils, made with 80% Roussanne and 15% Grenache blanc and 5% others.

Who wouldn't want a glass?

Restaurant | Famous Chef:

Chateau de Beaucastel

http://www.beaucastel.com/?langue=en

Châteaux of Bordeaux

Did you know that there are more than ten thousand Châteaux labels of Bordeaux wine? I am listing below the etymologies of my favourites. Many of these tales come courtesy of Kathleen Buckley of *The Wine Enthusiast*:

Ausone: named after Ausonius, the fourth century Latin poet and first known grower of Bordeaux wine. Ausonius' own villa was probably located at Bazas.

Bacchus: a title that reflects the owner Jean-Paul Grimal's legendary reputation for drinking.

Batailley: built near a battlefield (*champ de bataille*) where the French and English fought near the end of the Hundred Years War.

Beychevelle: name dating from the sixteenth century, when ships sailing up the Gironde River would lower their sails (*bacha velo* in the Gascon dialect) to honour the duke of Epernon, Jean-Louis Nogaret de la Valette, who was an admiral in France's navy. Though this story may be apocryphal, it is certainly true that de la Valette gave the estate its name.

Canon: in reference to the ships anchored on the Dordogne that habitually fired cannons from Fronsac hill in the sixteenth century. A rival history would have the estate acquiring its name from Jacques Kanon, the eighteenth-century owner who enlarged the Canon estate from a mere *clos* to the vineyards that we would recognize today.

Chasse-Spleen: from the wine's reputation to chase the blues away, a sobriquet given either by either Charles Baudelaire or Lord Byron, both of whom visited the estate. An oversight in the 1855 classification means that Chasse-Spleen's vintages only ever qualify as *cru bourgeois*, despite their frequent excellence.

Ducru-Beaucaillou: due to the beautiful pebbles running across the estate. This estate was known as Maucaillou (from *mauvais cailloux*, bad pebbles) in the eighteenth century. An early (and successful!) exercise in rebranding.

Haut-Brion: from *aubrion,* gravel mountain. According to fifteenth century records, Aubrion was also the name of the estate's manor house.

Lafite-Rothschild: Lafite comes from *la hite*, an old Gascon word for a 'little hill'. An amusingly pedestrian name for one of the world's greatest wines.

Lamothe du Prince Noir: named after the fourteenth-century "Black Prince," who lived here during the Hundred Years' War.

Latour: named after fortified towers that were built 600 years ago to deter pirates; however, the towers were square not round as on the label.

Montrose: meaning *pink mountain,* or perhaps – according to Clive Coates in his *Grands Vins: The Finest Chateaux of Bordeaux and their Wines* – it was taken from the heather (*mont-rose*) which covered the estate as recently as the nineteenth century.

Mylord: Madame Large, who owns the estate, claims the name comes from *Mille Louis d'Or*, which was the price paid for the estate in the eighteenth century.

Mouton-Rothschild: the word *mouton*, which means sheep in modern French; in Old French, however, *mouton* meant 'hill.'

Talbot: John Talbot commanded the English forces at Cavaillon, where the Brits lost Bordeaux for good, bringing the Hundred Years War nearer its close. The incongruous English name gives this estate a little romance.

Trottevieille: in reference to the old trotting lady who used to trot down the vineyard to hear news from the drivers of passing coaches.

I am sure they are hundreds more so don't hesitate to send them to me for the next tome.

Restaurant | Famous Chef:

Bordeaux wine website

http://www.bordeaux.com/Default.aspx?culture=en-US&country=OTHERS

CHILIES

My first experience of truly spicy food was in Thailand, when I was a management trainee at Le Meridien President in Bangkok. I will never forget the Pak Khlong Talat market, and the street food stalls nearby. I was especially taken with lemongrass and coriander, which were difficult to find in the Lyons of my youth. Thai cuisine is based on the balance of five fundamentals flavours: spicy, sour, sweet, salty and bitter. That year I got to know them all.

For lunch, I would sit down with the restaurant manager, who would tuck into a *larp gai*, or spicy minced chicken salad. He then would start sweating as hard as if he had run a marathon. When I questioned him about his extreme tastes, he would smile and say that the chilies left him impervious to Bangkok's steamy weather.

One of my favourite meals was *tom yam gung*, Thailand's famous hot and sour soup made with lemon grass, kaffir lime leaves, ginger, mushrooms, lime juice, coriander leaves, fish sauce, and – of course – loads of chilies. David Thompson, probably the West's foremost authority on Thai cuisine, has written that *tom yam* "encompasses a vast range of dishes, from the extremely basic to the highly complex – *tom* simply means to 'boil' and *yam* to 'mix' or 'toss together.'

In the streets where I ate, *tom yam* was served in aluminium hotpots with flames darting out of a hole in the centre. In Thailand, diners often cook the raw ingredients themselves, placing each shrimp, mushroom or bamboo shoot into the stock as it bubbled away. Seasoning the soup in the bowl gives the flavours a powerful immediacy, and also allows the diner to adjust for taste.

Spice warms the body up and sears your mouth until finally your tongue loses all sensation. A chemical reaction causes these effects: the peppers, or capsicum, increase body temperature, as a result of the chemical compound capsaicin. It is an irritant for humans, and produces a sensation of burning in any tissue with which it comes into contact. As one writer put it, "Chilli pungency is not technically a taste; it is the sensation of burning, controlled by the same mechanism that would let you know that someone had set your tongue on fire."

Chilli peppers can lower blood pressure, help the body digest starches, and increase saliva. They may also limit the multiplication of bacteria, which in hot climates is a quite useful side-effect. Chillies also produce sweat, which cools the body by evaporation. Christopher Columbus coined the word *pepper* when he first tasted chillies in the Caribbean, where they have been domesticated and eaten for around 6000 years. Columbus mistakenly thought the chilli was related to black peppercorns!

Chilli peppers differ in intensity: their potency is measured in Scoville Heat Units (SHU). A Mexican jalapeño rates 3,000 SHU, while India's Naga Jolokia stands at a fiery 1,000,000.

So now you know why curries are the perfect beach food!

Chin Chin

Champagne, corks popping, glasses clinking, people 'cheers-ing' as they look each other in the eyes. For me this custom is the essence of true hospitality: sharing a glass of champagne or wine among friends around an elegant table, whilst waiting for the meal to start. Maybe it's a birthday, a celebration, or a dinner between friends, but have you ever wondered why we follow this odd tradition of knocking two glasses together before drinking? Read on: it turns out that this seemingly happy custom has a sinister background.

During the Middle Ages, it was usual to deal with enemies – even if they were family or old friends – by poisoning their drinks. This practice was particularly popular among the most powerful families of Europe like the Borgias and the Medici. Catherine de Medici, Queen of France, was known for her regular use of poison in her "friends'" drinks.

To avoid being murdered by their supposed friends, people would pour a little bit of their own drink into the other person's glass and vice versa, meeting each other's eyes while doing so. The meaning was clear: 'if you try to poison me, you will also die'. With the passing of time, the pouring of the drinks became a ritual clinking of the glasses and today we keep this tradition without knowing its origins.

But before pronouncing these words, ensure there are no Japanese present, as the word *chin* means "penis" in Japanese. In other countries, you would say "Cheers," "Santé," "Salute," or "Salud," meaning health… in reference to the (hopefully) non-poisonous drink you are about to have.

And don't believe anyone who tells you that you must look into their eyes, lest you suffer ten years of bad sex! But the next time you share a drink, show your cultured sensibilities and diplomacy by looking the other person straight in the eyes. Then clink your glass against the other's glass, while savouring that moment.

Remember never to toast with water, as it is supposed to bring bad luck. According to an old naval superstition, the person to whom the toast is addressed will die by drowning! The expression "toast" comes from the sixteenth century, when the English used to add toasted bread to flavour their drinks!

Bottoms up!

Chocolate Cookies

The English word "cookie" comes from the Dutch *koekje* ("little cake"); Dutch immigrants brought the recipe with them to the United States. I ate my first chocolate chip cookie when I was seventeen. I had just finished high school, and had left Lyons for Fresno in California, where I planned to study for TOEFL, the English proficiency exam, which I needed to pass before studying at Lausanne. A recipe for chocolate chip cookies is the only thing I brought back from Fresno, apart from a Bible given to me by a beautiful but unobtainable woman. But that's another story for another book!

As one of its options, my language school offered cooking classes. That's where I learnt how to make these cookies. Delicious. I loved how the cookie, chocolate chips intact, would melt in your mouth when you ate it fresh from the oven. I made my dough from flour, butter, eggs, vanilla, baking soda and – of course – the famous chocolate chips.

Every year, an estimated seven *billion* chocolate chip cookies are sold in the US. Imagine how many more are eaten! Like many iconic recipes, the first chocolate chip cookie came about by mistake. It was invented by a lady called Ruth Wakefield in 1930 at the Toll House Inn in Massachusetts. One day she decided to make chocolate butter cookie (the obscurely named Butter Drop Do cookie) for the inn's boarders; as she was out of baker's chocolate, she broke up a bar of Nestle's semi-sweet chocolate instead. She thought that the chocolate would melt and swirl in the dough, but it did not: it kept its texture while the dough around it firmed up and turned creamy. But the recipe was so good, and her guests loved it so much, that she published the recipe in a Boston paper.

Wakefield called it Chocolate Crunch Cookie (CCC) and cut a contract with Nestlé, whose sales of semi-sweet chocolate had spiked as Wakefield's recipe was baked throughout the country. Nestlé could put the recipe on their chocolate bar, hence the Nestle Toll House Cookie recipe; in exchange, the company would supply her with free chocolate forever.

Sweet deal, Ruth!

Recipe:

Original chocolate cookie recipe from Ruth Wakefield

http://www.verybestbaking.com/recipes/specialty/nth-detail-occc.aspx

Chopsticks

Though a gastronomic paradise, Lyons in my youth had very few foreign restaurants; and the restaurants that existed were more gimmicky than good quality. Consequently I only learned how to use chopsticks when I went to Thailand in 1994 for my final internship at the Bangkok Méridien – despite much practice, it took me a while to become confident when using chopsticks, though eventually I could even pick up single grains of rice or green peas.

The English word "chopstick" comes from *chop chop*, which means "quick" in pidgin, the Chinese-English dialect that evolved from the seventeenth century in ports along China's Pacific coast where the English and the Chinese traded with each other.

Under China's Shang dynasty – while in Europe everyone could only eat with their bare hands or crude knives – China's population rapidly expanded. Forests were cut down to make way for cultivated land; fewer forests meant less wood, which meant that cooks had to be extremely frugal when using kindling. As a solution, the Chinese began cutting everything – from meat to vegetables – into very thin slices, which meant food cooked more quickly, thereby conserving wood.

Because wood existed in finite supply, furniture was expensive and rare. And when eating, an ancient Chinese needed to support the bowl in one hand, while picking up food with the other. Chopsticks were a simple but clever solution to the problem. Wielding chopsticks, people could deftly pick up the thin slices of food single-handed.

From the Tang dynasty onward, Chinese emperors used silver chopsticks, believing that the metal would change colour if it came into contact with poison!

During my time in Hong Kong, I carefully followed chopsticks etiquette: you cannot help yourself with your chopsticks directly from the sharing dish; never stick your chopsticks upright into a bowl of rice. Foreigners who fail to observe these rules are thought very uncouth.

CHOP CHOP!

Chowder

I have always been a great fan of soups and stews, and am quite happy with only soup for dinner, especially something I have made myself from organic vegetables cooked in a richly flavoured stock.

Reay Tannahill has claimed that chowder is the first truly American dish; it may even be the first truly American word – hence its importance to *The Curious Gourmand*. As you may have guessed, my appetite for etymologies is insatiable.

A chowder is a hearty soup containing salt pork, corn flour, ship's biscuit (as a thickener in place of flour) and onions. I first tried chowder in Edinburgh; during the bitter Scottish winters, I would eat soup every day, everything from The Balmoral's cock-a-leekie to Baxters chowder, which was my favourite tinned soup, along with the improbably tasty Highland Game with Cask Aged Sherry. Venison, hare, woodpigeon and pheasant in a can, but delicious.

The term chowder was first used in North America in the 1730s, and probably derives from the French word *chaudière*, which was an iron cooking pot that early French settlers brought with them when they moved to Newfoundland. These pioneers would toss the day's catch into their *chaudières* and toss in whatever vegetable was available. North American inns and taverns, which were forerunners of modern restaurants, would serve soups and 'chowders' to their guests. In fact, the word restaurant itself comes from the French word *restaurer,* 'to restore,' in reference to the rich soup served to wayfarers.

Chowder

In New England, pioneers adapted the Native American method of cooking clams: steamed on hot stones placed in water in a hollowed tree trunk. These little shellfish brought the tang of the sea to the chowder's combination of earthy vegetables and salt bacon.

So, the French contributed chowder; the English, apple pie; the Dutch, coleslaw; and the Germans, the hot dogs.

Many nations, one picnic.

Recipe:

Clam Chowder recipe

Restaurant | Famous Chef:

Dean & Deluca, pp. 38-9

Cocido

I came across this beautiful dish during my time in Madrid, Spain where it is considered *the* national plate. However, by writing this story I know that I will make myself a few enemies, since *cocido* has many variations, each hotly defended.

Cocido resembles the French pot-au-feu, a stew made with chickpeas, meat and vegetables, though the Spanish version originated with the Sephardic Jewish community: it was called *adafina* and cooked in an earthenware pot called an *olla*, one later replaced by the more pedestrian pressure cooker.

Madrid's *cocido* is made with beef, chickpeas, cabbage, carrots and turnips. It would be cooked overnight so that it could be eaten on the Sabbath, when work was forbidden. Later Marranos (a word that originally meaning 'pork eaters,' describing those Jews forced to convert to Christianity, though its meaning later degraded to 'pig') began adding chorizo and morcilla (blood sausage) to the dish.

The most important ingredient is the meat, which is chosen for diversity: salted meat, fresh meat, smoked sausage, and old hen. A proper *cocido* takes an entire day to cook, so that tough meat can become tender.

Cocido is supposed to be served in three courses (or *vuelco,* Spanish for 'overturn' as the pot had to be changed to serve each course and keep the ingredients separate*)*: first, broth with the *relleno* meatballs or matzoh balls; then vegetables; and finally, meat. Each *vuelco* varies by region: the Galician, for instance, calls for pork, while the Madrileno requires beef.

During the Spanish Inquisition, militant Catholics would roam Madrid, nostrils flared, to catch the scent of Jewish *adafina*. Some informants might even bring pork sausages to dinner, to test the host: if he added it to the stew, he was spared.

Cheap and earthy, *cocido* has always been popular in Madrid. Many restaurants and taverns around town offer *cocido* as a daily special on Tuesdays. I would often meet my friends Paz and Rafael de la Vega at El Puchero en la Calle Larra for my favourite Madrileno cocido.

Don't forget to eat it with Dijon mustard!

Recipe:

Cocido recipe

http://www.spain-recipes.com/cocido-recipe.html

Restaurant | Famous Chef:

Restaurante El Puchero, Madrid

http://www.elpuchero.com/

Cocktail

Every cocktail has a story. For me cocktails are about friendship; you choose the drink that reflects your mood: sour, sweet, fizzy, smooth or bubbly.

I often met my friend Frédéric Hermel at Le Cock, one of Madrid's most storied bars, where once Ernest Hemingway would meet Ava Gardner on the sly. Frédéric is a journalist whose work appears in both Spanish and French daily papers. Le Cock's bartender Fernando knew Frédéric well. One night, Frédéric came in, disconsolate. The bartender glanced at him and asked what he wanted. "Something bitter and strong. Like *life*," Frédéric said. Fernando fell to work, mixing a white spirit (gin or vodka), white rum, and *cynar* (artichoke liqueur), which gave it a slightly bitter tang. He poured the mixture into a martini glass and grated citrus zest over it. A few minutes later Fernando pushed the glass across the counter. Frédéric sipped; it was delicious. "How did you choose the ingredients?" asked Frédéric. "You looked tired, you looked worried, so I put a lot of sour stuff in with the Campari and gin." "What do you call it?" "…A Frédéric."

Fernando has since opened his own bar, Del Diego, on Madrid's Calle de la Reina. I encourage my readers to visit. Even if Fernando doesn't name a cocktail after you, you'll be inspired!

Originally cocktails were spirit-based, but the rising popularity of mixed drinks now means that the term includes wine-based drinks (traditionally known as punches or cups) and even non-alcoholic creations.

I cite here various legends about the origin of the name – all recounted in George Bishop's classic *The Booze Reader: A Soggy Saga of Man in His Cups* – many of which are a far cry from the sophisticated concoctions we enjoy today! Choose your favourite and call it true.

1. During the American Revolution, Betsy Flanagan, a tavern owner, stole a chicken from her English neighbour and served it to the American and French Revolutionary Army officers who were her customers. To celebrate her feat, she made mixed drinks decorated with the chicken's tail feathers, prompting one French officer to cry, "Vive le cocktail!"

2. In nineteenth century England, a cock-tail was shorthand for a woman of easy virtue, desirable but impure, and applied to British gin mixed with foreign ingredients (including ice).

3. Apparently in colonial Mexico, mixed drinks were stirred with spoons made from a local root called *cola de gallo* (cock tail).

4. An American tavern keeper used to pour leftover drinks into a rooster-shaped container; hard-up patrons could buy a glass of this cheap mixture which was dispensed from a tap at the rooster's tail.

5. The dregs (or tail-ends) of casks of different spirits were called cock tailings; all these leftovers were mixed and sold at a cheap price.

6. Antoine Peychaud, a pharmacist in nineteenth century New Orleans, created a mixed drink using his homemade bitters. Peychaud served it in an egg cup, known as a *coquetel* in French! Peychaud's bitters are still an integral ingredient in a Sazerac, thought by many to be the first cocktail ever invented (see *Absinthe*).

Fancy a drink?

Recipe:

The Frédéric

Restaurants | Famous Chefs:

Del Diego, Madrid

http://www.worldsbestbars.com/city/madrid/del-diego-madrid.htm

Le Cock, Madrid

http://www.worldsbestbars.com/city/madrid/bar-cock-madrid.htm

COFFEE

As a child, I loved waking up to the smell of brewing coffee; it remains one of my favourite memories of the holidays.

Coffee originated in Ethiopia, where we find the first written reference to it in the work of a tenth century Arabian doctor. Berries were eaten whole. Mixed with fat and then fermented, the pulp was then used for a drink that was classed as a type of wine. By the thirteenth century, the beans were cleaned and roasted before being infused, much like today's coffee.

The word *coffee* comes from the Turkish *kahveh*, which itself comes from Arabic *qahwah* ('wine'). The Dervishes, known for chanting and whirling in an ecstatic frenzy until they collapsed, favoured coffee, which they felt focused the mind during extended periods of prayer.

Muslim pilgrims spread the use of coffee throughout the Middle East and North Africa. Café Procope, the first coffee house in France, was founded in 1686. Still flourishing, it is one of my favourite Parisian cafés. I opened a restaurant called Alcazar for Sir Terence Conran on the same street in St Germain-des-Prés in the Sixth Arrondissement. While we renovated Alcazar, I would step across to Procope for my morning café.

I have lived in over eleven countries and have discovered in each a particular custom regarding coffee consumption. I have to say that it was Spain that surprised me the most, just for the sheer variety of coffee available: *café solo, cortado* (espresso and milk), *con leche* (coffee with milk), *con leche templada* (with milk at room temperature), *cappuccino, bombon* (with condensed milk), *con hielo* (ice coffee), *mocha* (with milk

+ chocolate powder), *carajillo* (with brandy or rum), *descaffeinado*…

I personally drink black coffee for breakfast. I prefer it made in the Italian coffee pot known as a *macchinetta,* or Moka pot. These little stove top espresso coffee makers have water inside the base, ground coffee in a metal filter placed on top, and the metal chamber above, where the coffee is collected. The steam forces the boiling water up through the ground coffee and then into the chamber.

Un café, s'il vous plait!

Restaurant | Famous Chef:

Procope, Paris

http://www.procope.com/

Cordon Bleu

I have always heard the expression *being a cordon bleu* to describe talented chefs. Julia Child is one of the school's famous alumna; others include New York restaurateur Mario Batali (who left before attaining his diploma), Nathalie Dupree, and Giada de Laurentiis, the TV host and chef.

The Cordon bleu was an order created by King Henry III in 1578 as L'Ordre des Chevaliers du Saint Esprit. To be eligible, a man had to be Roman Catholic and of noble rank. The symbol of the order is a Maltese cross with a dove and fleur-de-lis between each triangle. But most important was the blue ribbon that the Cross of the Holy Spirit hung on; those blue ribbons quickly became signs of the highest royal distinction. The dinners served to *les Cordons-bleus* at their ceremonial meetings were "legendary."

By the eighteenth century, the term was particularly associated with food, either because a Saint Cyr school was particularly associated with cooking, and its students wore blue sashes; or because Madame du Barry's *cuisinière* so impressed Louis XV, that du Barry suggested he award her a *Cordon-bleu*. Whatever the term's origin, by 1827 a cookbook was published called *Le Cordon bleu ou nouvelle cuisinière bourgeoise*. Today the ribbons have gone, and only the expression related to excellence in cuisine remains.

The Cointreau group owns around thirty Cordon Bleu schools throughout the world. The expression 'Cordon Bleu' also gave its name to a dish in Austria (Wiener schnitzel), a veal escalope coated with breadcrumbs and then fried and served with a lemon wedge.

For me the Cordon Bleu has poignant associations, as one of my good friends from Lausanne, Nathalie de Montalembert, was a graduate of the Cordon Bleu school. Nathalie was tall, with dark hair and eyes, and had a sort of inner light that made her loved by her classmates. When she was just twenty years old, Nathalie fell from a boat into the Ardèche River and drowned.

Among my fondest memories of Lausanne are the parties Nathalie and I attended at the student-run restaurant and bar called La Ferme. We would play pool and serve food from our own countries, whether Spanish, German, French, or Italian. Nathalie, who was quite a skilled cook, would make Argentinian empanadas. Though simple, they were delicious; she knew that technical proficiency wasn't enough, that a good meal must reflect the soul of the person who makes it.

…Are you a Cordon Bleu?

Restaurant | Famous Chef:

Cordon Bleu school

http://www.cordonbleu.edu/

Cosmopolitan

For me the Cosmopolitan is the cocktail that represents New York. It is funny how so many of the world's great cities have their own signature cocktails: Singapore's Singapore Sling, New York's Manhattan, and the Daiquiri and the Mojito from Havana, Cuba …

The Cosmopolitan became popular thanks to the stars of *Sex in the City*. The cocktail is made with vodka, orange liqueur, cranberry juice and lime juice served in a Martini glass with an orange zest. Its beautiful pink colour might explain why men rarely go for it (at least in public). Mixologist Dale De Groff, called the Cocktail King, became famous for serving it to Carrie Bradshaw and her friends.

Similar drinks have been around for a while, including the Kamikaze (vodka, orange liqueur and fresh lime) and the Cape Codder (vodka and cranberry juice on the rocks with a wedge of lime).

But the Cosmopolitan's creation is generally credited to a Florida bartender named Cheryl Cook. In the 1980s she noticed that many of her customers seemed to be ordering martinis more for the iconic glass than for its contents. She created the Cosmopolitan to give them something more palatable to sip from a martini glass. The drink was an instant hit and its popularity spread across the United States. The version enjoyed today was bartender Toby Ceccini's take on the Cosmopolitan (or Cosmo to its fans) at the Odeon in New York.

Sex and the City inspired a few other cocktail fads, including the Tartini (raspberry vodka, cranberry juice, Chambord and lime) and the Ruby (vodka and ruby grapefruit juice), but they were short-lived compared to the enduring appeal of the Cosmo.

At the Hong Kong Mandarin Oriental, we served a molecular version of the Cosmopolitan; over each cocktail, floated a cloud of cranberry foam made with a siphon filled with cranberry juice and gelatine.

Carrie said it best: "Hi, I'd like a cheeseburger, large fries and a Cosmopolitan."

Recipe:	**Restaurant	Famous Chef:**
Sex and the City cosmopolitan recipe	Mbar, Mandarin Oriental, Hong Kong
http://ohgo.sh/archive/sex-and-the-city-the-cosmopolitan/	http://www.mandarinoriental.com/hongkong/dining/bars_and_lounge/m_bar/

Crêpes Suzette

This is a classic dessert created by mistake, much like the Tarte Tatin. I first heard this story from Edouard Ettedgui, ex CEO of Mandarin Oriental Hotel Group.

For those not familiar with this dish, it consists in a crêpe with caramelized sugar, orange juice, orange peel and Grand Marnier (orange liqueur) flambéed so the alcohol evaporates and only the flavour remains. The concentrated syrup is then poured over the crêpe.

It is a dessert that stirs passions: one customer was so incensed at the Mandarin Grill + Bar's deconstructed interpretation of this classic, that he wrote Mr. Ettedgui a furious letter demanding "the cook responsible be flogged."

In 1895, Henri Charpentier, a teenage waiter, was preparing dessert for England's future King Edward VII, then the Prince of Wales, who had come to dine at the Monaco's Café de Paris. His memoirs (*Life* à *La Henri*) describe what happened:

"It was quite by accident as I worked in front of a chafing dish that the cordials caught fire. I thought I was ruined. The Prince and his friends were waiting. How could I begin all over? I tasted it. It was, I thought, the most delicious melody of sweet flavours I had ever tasted. I still think so. That accident of the flame was precisely what was needed to bring all those various instruments into one harmony of taste... He ate the pancakes with a fork; but he used a spoon to capture the remaining syrup. He asked me the name of that which he had eaten with so much relish. I told him it was to be called Crêpe Princesse. He recognized that the pancake controlled the gender and that this was a compliment designed for him; but he protested with mock ferocity that there was a lady present. She was alert and rose to her feet and holding her little skirt wide with her hands she made him a curtsey. "Will you," said His Majesty, "change Crêpe Princesse to Crêpe Suzette?" Thus, was born and baptized this confection, one taste of which, I really believe, would reform a cannibal into a civilized gentleman. The next day I received a present from the Prince, a jewelled ring, a panama hat and a cane."

Sadly, as so often happens with pretty stories, this one is disputed; *Larousse* dismisses the Charpentier's claims, arguing that he would not have been chosen to serve the prince, with more senior staff present. My feeling is that if this story isn't true, it ought to be.

Whatever the truth, Charpentier dined out on the story for the rest of his life!

Recipe:

Crêpe Suzette classic recipe

http://www.bbc.co.uk/food/recipes/classiccrepessuzette_66236

Restaurant | Famous Chef:

Mandarin Grill + Bar, Hong Kong

http://www.mandarinoriental.com/hongkong/dining/restaurants/mandarin_grill/

CROISSANT

When people dream of Paris, they imagine many things; but most will picture the terrace of the famous Les Deux Magots, crowded with people enjoying their morning coffee, dipping a croissant in it.

Croissants are made from a yeast-based dough layered with butter, rolled and folded several times to create *pâte feuilletée* (puff pastry). An iconic symbol of French food, the croissant ('crescent' in English) is a surprisingly recent addition to my country's ancient cuisine. The earliest mention of the croissant as we know it occurs only in 1906, with Auguste Colombie's *Nouvelle Encyclopédie culinaire: La Cuisine Bourgeoise, La Pâtisserie Bourgeoise*. But even that recipe would not be one we recognize today, since it consisted only of yeast-raised bread (albeit in a crescent shape); only in the 1920s did the familiar laminated dough come about, with the delightful flaky melting quality we know now.

The 1938 edition of *Larousse gastronomique* mistakenly cited the Viennese as its creators, baking the first crescent pastries to celebrate the 1683 defeat of Ottoman siege. The story went that Vienna's bakers heard the Turks tunnelling and sounded the alarm by baking crescents (in reference to the Turkish flags). Then, when the Turks fled, they abandoned a huge stock of coffee. One battle hero, Kulyesiski, opened the first café in Vienna.

This story has, however, been refuted as a fairy tale, though I still find it charming and plan to tell it to my children as alternative history! Recently the culinary writer Jim Chevallier claims that August Zang, an

Austrian officer, introduced the croissant's precursor, the *kipfer*, to Paris in the 1830s. (The kipfer was a crescent shaped roll that was usually filled with nuts or jam, to Paris in the 1830s.) Zang's Boulangerie Viennoise opened in la Rue de Richelieu; hence the expression "viennoiserie" referring to baked goods made from a yeast leavened dough with some additional ingredients such as butter, cream, milk (see *Brunch*).

Wherever it came from, the croissant belongs to France now, and we're ceding it to no one!

Restaurants | Famous Chefs:

Boulangerie Viennoise, Paris

http://en.wikipedia.org/wiki/File:Boulangerie_Viennoise_formerly_Zang's_-_1909.jpg

Les Deux Magots, Paris

http://www.lesdeuxmagots.fr/

Croque-Monsieur

The croque-monsieur reminds me of Parisian cafés, where I love to sit outside watching the passers-by; wondering about their lives, I eat a croque-monsieur and a salad.

This recipe at least is one whose French origins are incontestable. The croque-monsieur consists of a crispy sandwich with ham and melted cheese on top: Anne Willan once fairly described it as the hamburger of France, since it can be found in bars and cafés from Calais to Marseille.

The croque-monsieur first appeared in a Parisian café around 1910. The onomatopoeic word *croque* means *crunch*; monsieur means – of course – mister.

According to tradition, French workers during the Industrial Revolution would bring lunch with them to the factory. They would leave their ham and Gruyère cheese sandwiches near a radiator so the cheese could melt. Later a chef must have decided to pan fry the bread to make it crispy. With butter you get a brown colour; with olive oil, a golden one.

There are many other versions of the croque-monsieur, the most popular being its female counterpart, the croque-madame, which crowns a croque-monsieur with a fried egg resembling a lady's hat.

This sandwich was very popular during the late 1970s and the 1980s. When my mother came back late from work, she would open a packet of ready-made croque-monsieurs. She tossed them in a hot pan until the cheese melted and got crispy. Cheap and cheerful cuisine.

The croquet-monsieur also has regional variations: le croque-Provençal (tomato), le croque-auvergnat (blue cheese from Auvergne), and in Savoy, croque-tartiflette (potato and Reblochon cheese) …

Recipe:	**Restaurant	Famous Chef:**
Croque Monsieur recipe	Café Flore, Paris
http://simplyrecipes.com/recipes/croque_monsieur_ham_and_cheese_sandwich/	http://www.cafedeflore.fr/

CRYING ONION

Every child has seen his mother crying while slicing onions. I remember asking mine why was she crying? I was somewhat older before I understood that slicing onions brings on tears.

There is a scientific reason for my mother's tears: onion cells contain allyl enzymes that are released when the onion is cut. These enzymes react with the air by transforming into allyl sulphite, an irritant and volatile substance which escapes in form of gas and irritates the tear ducts.

We cry because our eyes are trying to eliminate the allyl by rinsing it out. Unfortunately, the water combined with allyl sulphite gases then turns into hydrogen sulphide, sulphur dioxide, and sulfuric acid, further irritants. It is, as Harold McGee says, "a very effective molecular bomb"!

The word *onion* comes from the Latin *unio*, meaning 'single white pearl.' Onions belong to the Allium family, which include garlic, too; botanists call class them as *Allium cepa,* which includes all common western globe onions that have single bulbs.

It was during my chef's apprenticeship at the Hotel du Rhône in Geneva (now the Mandarin Oriental) that I learnt how to prevent the crying process. You can soak the onion in water for almost an hour to dilute the sulphite; or freeze it for 10 minutes; ventilate the room so the allyl sulphite can escape; or light a candle to burn away the fumes. It is also said that chewing gum, or eating a piece of bread helps, though I myself have never tried those stratagems.

I also would like to share with you a few tips from Mamie on how to keep the onions: they should be stored away from the sun and humidity; keep them in a ventilated room. Should they start showing green shoots, do not throw the onion away: use it in salads as a substitute for chives.

Onions don't cry!

Restaurant | Famous Chef:

Hotel du Rhône, Geneva

http://www.mandarinoriental.com/geneva/?kw=hotel-du-rhone&htl=MOGVA&eng=goog&src=ppc

Dai Pai Dong

A dai pai dong is an open-air food stall usually located in a small alley off one of Hong Kong's main streets. It was a friend who brought me to my first dai pai dong – Shing Kee on Graham Street – after he himself fell in love with its vibrant Cantonese flavours (and great prices). Shing Kee was only five minutes' walk and a world away from the Mandarin's austerely elegant bars and cafés. At first, I never knew its name; like other Hong Kongers, we just knew where it was. I would order whatever the staff recommended, though of course I had my favourite dishes, especially chicken or fish in black bean sauce.

On my first visit to Shing Kee, I was overwhelmed by sensations: the fragrant smells, the bright colours, the cacophony of voices. The tables and chairs are the kind of furniture you would expect at the beach: they are made of plastic and plastered with beer advertisements. Once I'd sat down, I was served hot tea; all around me people were sanitizing plastic chopsticks in their teacups. The restaurant is a family affair, with each member having a particular duty. The chef works over his wok despite extremely high temperatures (there is no means of heat extractions); the 'slicer,' or sous-chef, who does the prep work; the waiter; the runner who collects dirty plates and cutlery in a plastic bucket; and finally, the cleaner, who dumps everything into an enormous rubbish bin, and who washes dishes and pots before rinsing them. It is a very well-oiled machine, by my observation!

I recommend that every visitor to Hong Kong try a dai pai dong. The city's neon shop signs light your meal; you eat while the city roars around you and the food sizzles away on the chef's wok.

Dai pai dong began springing up in Hong Kong during the nineteenth century. The numbers of dai pai dong increased exponentially, however after WW2, when the government issued the now famous Big License (in reference to a stall's size): the name Dai Pai Dong translates as "large-license stall."

In recent years, though, citing traffic issues, the city's Food and Environmental Hygiene Department began buying back the licenses, which only a spouse can inherit. There are currently only 28 official dai pai dong in Hong Kong, and they are slated to disappear.

Find one and fall to before they all vanish!

Restaurant | Famous Chef:

Shing Kee, Hong Kong

http://www.discoverhongkong.com/tramguide/eng/merchant_detail.jsp?spot_id=40

Daube of Beef

Daubes always put me in mind of winter dinners when fireplaces are lit against the bitter cold that seeps in around December. Another classical French dish that originated in Provence, the daube is an iconic stew made with beef marinated in red wine, vegetables, garlic and herbs of Provence. A daube is one meal in a pot, whose flavours mingle and meat softens after 24-48 hours of marinating and cooking.

The word "daube" comes from the Spanish *adobar*, 'to marinate.' In Provence during the bullfight season, it was customary to use meat of bulls killed in the ring for the daube. It is often served with pasta or mashed potatoes – anything to soak up the sauces!

A daube is traditionally prepared in a daubière, a large casserole, made either from copper or terracotta, but one whose thin neck retards evaporation. The old people in Provence tell a funny story about how the daubière should never be cleaned. According to tradition, the pot is left to dry on top of a gas heater, so that the leftover sauce becomes a sort of thin crust whose flavours are then transferred to the daubière.

A proper daube is one that, as Patricia Wells says, "focuses not on the accompanying sauce or vegetables but on the meat, fish, or poultry that is slowly simmered to create a potful of complex, concentrated flavours." It may afterward be served with a *gremolata*, a chutney of garlic, parsley, and lemon zest.

I will pass on to you a few of my grandmother's tips for making the most delicious daubes: use beef morsels that are fibrous and fatty. Cook your daube over a wood fire, and if you can, in a *daubière*. Pair the dish with the same red wine you used for the marinade. And finally: make enough for leftovers, since daubes just get better and better with each reheating.

The best daube I have ever had was in Le Bistrot du Paradou in Maussane les Alpilles. That bistro was formerly a post office in 1832, is now run by Mireille and Jean-Louis Pons. Its four-course set price menu is deceptively simple, containing only the dish of the day, with a bottle of red wine already placed on the table.

Next time you are cold on a dark day in mid-winter and find yourself hungry, remember that beef daube is the best defence against the cold.

Recipe:	**Restaurant	Famous Chef:**
Daube provençale	675-6

Dim Sum

One of my favorite restaurants in Hong Kong is the Luk Yu Teahouse on Stanley Street, which still has its original Art Deco fittings of brass and rosewood. It is famous for its delicious dim sum and the abrupt manners of its waiters. David Tang – the owner of Hong Kong's China Club and founder of Shanghai Tang – has been going for years; his great-grandfather took tea there every day in the same cypress wood booth where David Tang now eats.

Dim sum translates as "touch the heart," or "fill the gap." It includes dumplings, rice noodle, and *shaomai* – buns made with beef, pork, shrimp, vegetables or even fruit. The ingredients may be steamed, fried, or deep-fried. Each steamer or plate usually comes with portions of three or four. In Hong Kong, drinking tea and eating dim sum together is known as Yum Cha ("tea drinking"). Chefs undergo years of apprenticeship to learn the vast repertoire of dishes: one expert claims that Cantonese dim sum encompasses more than a thousand varieties, though most restaurants will specialize in only a hundred. Westerners are most familiar with Cantonese dim sum, but China's northern regions have their own unique dishes.

Dim sum originated with the caravanserai tea houses of the Tang Dynasty (618-907), when travellers would stop to rest, sip tea and have a snack – consequently 'touching the heart,' rather than cramming the stomach. By the twelfth century, dim sum had evolved into the forms and names we use today: little prawn dumplings, bamboo leaf packets, mooncakes, spring rolls, and sausage *shaobing*. Records of the Song Dynasty's capital Hangzhou include long lists of dim sum sold in the city's taverns and wine houses, and there "is no reason to believe that the recipes have changed to any significant degree in the intervening six hundred years… [though] there were many more buns, pies and cakes listed, but since their names are no longer in common usage, they are not easy to identify," write May Huang Man-Hui and Margaret Leeming. "This is rather a shame, since 'gold orange-juice cake' sounds very inviting and the name 'one inside the other magic peaches' is intriguing." But the culinary traditions are constantly evolving modern menus include Western ingredients like foie gras dumplings and quail eggs.

In my opinion, the best Dim Sum restaurant in London is Min Jiang at the Royal Garden Hotel near Hyde Park south corner.

It should be obvious that you cannot order dim sum in the evening, unless you want to look like a fool!

Recipe:	**Restaurant	Famous Chef:**
Shaomai recipe	Luk Yu Teahouse, Hong Kong
http://www.epicurean.com/featured/shrimp-shao-mai-recipe.html	http://www.timeout.com.hk/restaurants-bars/top-100/1145/luk-yu-tea-house.html

Dom Perignon | Dom Ruinart | La Grande Dame | Cristal Roederer

Any connoisseur of Champagne will have intimate knowledge of Dom Pérignon, Dom Ruinart, La Grande Dame and Cristal Roederer. But who were those two Doms? Who was the Lady? And why are certain bottles called *Cristal*?

Dom Pérignon was the Benedictine monk often credited with inventing the sparkling wine now known as Champagne. Cellar master at the Abbey of Hautvilliers near Épernay, Dom Pérignon introduced innovative practices that greatly improved the quality of his abbey's wines, and which have influenced modern viniculture: "severe pruning, low yields, and careful harvesting." Dom Pérignon also experimented with producing white wine from black grapes like the Pinot Noir, since the chance of exploding bottles was lesser with black grapes, because secondary fermentation was less likely. Dom Pérignon also tinkered with reducing the maceration process. *The Oxford Companion to Wine* asserts that Pérignon deserves his place in the history books for those reasons, rather than as the father of Champagne, acidly observing that title "is the stuff of fairy-tales: the transition from still to sparkling wine was an evolutionary process rather than a dramatic discovery on the part of one man." Recent research has credited the English physician and scientist Christopher Merret as the first to document how adding sugar affected sparkling wines. But whatever the truth, Dom Pérignon has achieved immortality through the association of his name with the most prestigious of *cuvées*. Dom Pérignon is now part of the Moët & Chandon group.

Dom Pérignon was also indirectly associated with the founding of the oldest established Champagne house. His friend and fellow Benedictine, Dom Thierry Ruinart, encouraged his brother and nephew (both named Nicolas Ruinart) to find the House of Ruinart in 1729, one year after Louis XV decreed that champagne could be bottled rather than transported in casks. The glass, of course, preserved the sparkle created during fermentation would be preserved. Like Dom Pérignon, the Ruinart label also belongs to the Moët & Chandon group.

Philippe Clicquot-Muiron established the house which became Veuve Clicquot. Philippe spent twenty years building up the house, intending to leave it to his son François. But when François died early, his widow (*veuve*) Barbe-Nicole Clicquot-Ponsardin took over, as Philippe was by then too elderly to manage the vineyards himself. Nicole quickly established her wine within the European royal courts, focusing on Russia, and took the surname of "La Grande Dame" – a name that now refers to Clicquot's *prestige cuvée*. La Dame is best remembered, though, for instituting the system of *remuage*, which clarifies the sparkling wines from the yeast sediment that formed during secondary fermentation. Nicole and her *chef de caves,* Antoine Müller, designed special wooden racks on which the Champagne bottles could be balanced, neck downward, at an angle of 45°. Each day the wines were rotated and tilted, so that the sediment would collect just behind the cork. Thanks to the vision of la Grande Dame, sparkling wine became clear, translucent.

Cristal represented what has been called the first ever *prestige cuvée* (a producer's best blended Champagne). It was first produced by Louis Roederer and bottled for Russia's Alexander II. The tsar was offended that the Champagne he drank, its bottles "swathed in white linen," looked like his courtiers'; so, in 1876 Roederer called in a Flemish master glassmaker

Dom Perignon | Dom Ruinart | La Grande Dame | Cristal Roederer

who crafted a bottle with a flat bottom, of clear lead crystal. This *cuvee* was only for the tsar's table.

Other houses carry the name of their founders: Krug, Moët & Chandon, Laurent-Perrier, Pol Roger, Taittinger and Bollinger.

As Dom Pérignon said: 'Come quickly, I am drinking the stars…'

Restaurants | Famous Chefs:

http://www.domperignon.com/

http://www.ruinart.com/#//index.php

http://www.veuve-clicquot.com/fr/selection/la-grande-dame

http://www.champagne-roederer.com/modules/fiches_techniques/pdf/en/cristal_2002.pdf

Dragon Beard Candy

The first Chinese New Year I spent in Hong Kong I discovered a wonderful sweet that I had never seen before: dragon beard candy. Its thin consistency reminded me of cotton candy. The Mandarin Oriental was serving it out free of charge in the lobby; intrigued, I asked what it was. The substance was so strange - threads of sugar that came away in your hand. If cotton candy is like a cloud, dragon beard resembles a spool of thread, a ball.

Chinese confectioners make dragon beard by boiling solidified sugar until it becomes elastic. Once the candy turns into a torus, it is pulled and folded over itself, and the number of strands after each repetition is tripled. The 'beard' is then cut in small pieces, wrapped around crushed peanuts and covered in flour, to stop the strands from sticking together.

The first Dragon Beard candy was crafted almost two millennia ago, when one of the emperor's chefs spun myriad malt sugar threads into a fragile whole. The emperor became so fond of this sweet that he himself named it. Dragon Beard is served at dinner parties as a little after-meal treat; it may also be given as a small present for weddings, birthdays, and holidays.

I always recommended that my visitors request Dragon Beard candy from Lei Garden in Hong Kong's International Finance Centre, as I thought their version was particularly delicious and beautifully made. Lei Garden belongs to a restaurant group which has five Michelin stars among only nine restaurants. Meanwhile this ancient candy has been

Dragon Beard Candy

revived through on-line interest: a website called Bamboo Garden has built up a reputation for quality confections.

A word to the wise: don't try to count the strands: there are around three thousand in each candy! And eat fast: dragon beard is so sensitive to moisture and humidity that even a single hour after its creation, the candy gets sticky, and its delicate texture disappears.

Recipe:

Dragon Beard recipe video

http://www.youtube.com/watch?v=UbXj4jte7C8l

Restaurant | Famous Chef:

http://www.bamboogarden.com.hk/en/index.html

Dudu

There are a few select teachers in the École Hotelière de Lausanne who have inspired generations of students, me among them, with the vision of what a restaurant can be, both for those of us who create the experience and for the customers who enjoy it. No one inspired us more than Vladimir Durussel – known as Dudu to his protégés – who was not only a chef but also an actor and the author of *L'Étude, Redaction et Planification des Menus* (*The Study, Writing and Planning of Menus*). My own book would not exist without Dudu.

What are the protocols for writing a menu? Does the shellfish course come before or after meat? What are the origins of old-fashioned sauces (vichyssoise, Dugléré, beurre Café de Paris)? These questions may now be regarded as Old School at best and obsolete at worst, but Vladimir Durussel taught his students how elegant tradition could be.

Not a day goes by when I do not think of my teacher. Dudu insisted that we write Beef Stroganoff, not *Stroganov*; and that while either châteaubriant or chateaubriand would do, the second spelling is superior, as the first refers to the French aristocratic family, while the dish was named in honour of the famous writer: Chateaubriand reputedly would work for free in exchange for a double cut of meat.

Later I learned from Pierre Gagnaire that even the punctuation on a menu can have significance. For instance, a comma signifies that a separate ingredient is included with a dish's main component, while a semicolon indicates that the ingredient that follows it is served as a garnish with a separate dish. Finally, when Gagnaire starts a second line within the same paragraph, he is indicating that a satellite dish contains the main ingredient, though it will be prepared in a different manner.

For his menus, Chef Uwe Opocensky invents titles like 'flowerpot' and 'fire' – names that no customer would associate with a meal. Uwe uses no verbs or adverbs. This is culinary writing for the twenty-first century: the language of menus has been stripped down from the days of huge menus when the text was written almost like a prose poem.

At Soho House every time I was visiting a site, I would check the menus to ensure that they were written properly. I became obsessed by it and so was Nick Jones.

We miss you Dudu.

Restaurant | Famous Chef:

Vladimir Durussel book

http://www.iscahm.com/news/ch_part01e.htm

Easter Egg

As a child, I loved to hunt for Easter eggs. I remember the excitement of waking up early in my parents' house and vying with my sisters to find the most chocolate eggs and bunnies that my parents had hidden underneath our garden's pine trees.

The English word Easter comes from Eostre, the Anglo-Saxon goddess of Spring. Eostre loved children and used to practice magic to entertain them. One day a songbird fluttered down her hand, and she transformed it into a rabbit.

The compassionate children, though, begged Eostre to reverse her spell when they saw the poor animal scared and shivering. But the goddess' powers were unequal to the task, except in the spring, when her strength is at its zenith. The rabbit then briefly returns to its bird-form, and lays eggs. The egg was a pagan symbol of rebirth; this ancient belief has survived into modern times, albeit in diluted form.

The tradition of the Easter egg seems to have its origins with Lent, the period lasting 40 days (the length of time Christians believe that Jesus fasted in the desert). During Lent, believers are forbidden from eating meat and dairy products – including eggs (see *Carnival*). For Easter, they were back on the menu!

The tradition of decorating eggs comes from the Slavic countries of central Europe, where during ancient times, a sun god called Dazhboh was worshipped as the source of all life. The bedizened eggs, called *pysanka*, were considered to be talismans and magical objects. In Russia, children

Easter Egg

would bring these eggs to church during the Easter service to receive the priest's blessing: this peasant tradition continued in a more refined and luxurious form when Alexander III commissioned the first imperial egg in 1885. Crafted by Carl Fabergé, the jeweller from Saint Petersburg, it was called 'the Hen Egg.' This object probably also marked the twentieth anniversary of Alexander's betrothal to his wife. Fabergé become the court supplier and made an Easter egg every year, though each masterpiece took more than twelve months to create.

The most amazing Easter eggs I have seen were created by the famous Spanish pastry chef, Oriol Balaguer. His eggs are sculptures with names like 'Atomic' and 'Clown.'

Easter surprise!

Recipe:

Fabergé eggs

http://www.mieks.com/faberge-en/index.htm

Restaurant | Famous Chef:

Oriol Balaguer

http://www.oriolbalaguer.com/

Finger Tapping

When I first arrived in Hong Kong, I visited many teahouses. I noted with some curiosity how customers would tap the table with their fingers. After close observation, I realized that any customer whose teacups were refilled would acknowledge and thank the waiter by using his three middle fingers to tap the table.

Still practiced in southern China, finger tapping shows gratitude to someone for pouring tea. The custom dates back to the Qing Dynasty (1644-1912), when an emperor (reputedly the great Qianlong) amused himself by traveling in disguise throughout China; only his entourage would know his true identity. The emperor permitted his companions to show respect by using three fingers to tap on the table rather than kowtow (kneeling prostrate, forehead to the ground), which would have given ruined his disguise, since the kowtow at its most formal was practiced only for the imperial family.

The three fingers represent a discreet bow: with knuckles crooked against the table, the middle finger stands in for the bowed head, while the two external fingers serve as the bent arms. The gesture is completely discreet; the untrained eye will miss it altogether.

But finger tapping is not the only custom you can observe in a Chinese tea house. If you want your teapot refilled, you must leave the pot's lid open. You may also angle the lid on a diagonal, balance it on the handle, or leave it off altogether. You rate the quality of a restaurant's service by timing how long it takes the waiter to refill your pot.

Finger Tapping

An urban myth claims to account for this custom. Once upon a time, a young student kept a beautiful bird inside a special teapot which he carried with him everywhere, so much did he love the bird.

But one day the student brought this unorthodox birdcage to a restaurant where a waiter lifted its lid by mistake; the bird flew out; she was gone forever. The student complained bitterly. Ever since, all Hong Kong teahouses wait for the customer's signal – lifting the lid – before refilling tea.

The story reminds me of a protocol practiced among French billiard players, when spectators snap their fingers rather than clapping, which prevents breaking the players' concentration.

Restaurant | Famous Chef:

China Tee Club, Hong Kong

http://www.chinateeclub.com.hk/

Forbidden Fruit

A friend, once gave me a great book called *In the Devil's Garden: A Sinful History of Forbidden Fruit*, by Stewart Lee Allen; I recommend it to all my readers. In it, Allen treats culinary history and geography as reflected by the Seven Deadly Sins. You will never look at your food the same way again, that's for sure!

"And the Lord God commanded Adam, saying, 'Of every tree of the garden thou mayest freely eat, but of the tree of the knowledge of good and evil, thou shalt not eat of it: for in the day that thou eatest thereof, thou shalt surely die…'"

But the food was so irresistible, so delicious, that Adam and his wife Eve ignored God's injunction; they ate, lost their innocence, and were exiled from the Garden of Eden. Imagine world cuisine if they had not: no Tarte Tatin! No Charlotte à la Milanese (Apple Charlotte)! No Calvados…!

Christians have often identified the apple as the Forbidden Fruit, since its juice is so sweet that it supposedly could distract the faithful from the Word of God, and the tartness of its finish gave away the devil's influence, since those almost bitter flavours suggest poison. The apple's red skin hinted at a beautiful woman's luscious lips; its flesh is white like her teeth and sensuous like her skin. Only the devil could have made the apple so crisp, so delectable, unlike other fruits that soften and deliquesce, as they grow ripe.

If you slice the apple in half, vertically, the apple core looks like a woman's sex; when cut in half, horizontally, the pattern of seeds resembles a five-pointed star, or pentagram, which is the devil's ultimate symbol.

In contrast to the Catholic tradition, which distrusts sensual pleasures, the Celts revered the apple; their paradise was called *Insula Avallonis*, or Island of the Apples...

For those who share my love of apples, I also recommend *An Apple A Week,* by Sir David Tang. The book is a collection of articles that Tang published in the *Apple Daily* newspaper from 2004–06. Tang was a rare Hong Konger who would speak about Hong Kong's flaws as well as its strengths. We owe Sir David the creation of the beautiful China Club: I think of it as the Colombe d'Or's counterpart in Asia - its collection of contemporary Chinese art is unparalleled in Hong Kong.

Restaurant | Famous Chef:

China Club, Hong Kong

http://www.tripadvisor.com/Restaurant_Review-g294217-d786802-Reviews-China_Club-Hong_Kong_Hong_Kong_Region.html

The Fork

Have you ever wondered about the origins of the fork? Common during the classical era – Homer mentions their use in *The Odyssey* – the first forks, which had only two tines, were used for serving rather than eating. And where a knife or a spoon failed, fingers would do.

The Byzantine princess Teodora Ducas brought the first fork to Europe in the eleventh century, when she married the Venetian doge Domenico Selvo. The Italian clerics were suspicious of her manners, especially her use of 'diabolical' forks, which were believed to resemble a satanic implement. When the princess died of plague, some pious but pitiless Italians felt that divine retribution had struck her down. In Europe, the fork's reputation as a licentious implement lasted for hundreds of years: despite its utility, the fork was slow to catch on. In 1562, Paolo Veronese's *Marriage at Cana* depicts a courtesan with a fork angled seductively at the corner of her mouth. France's Henri III was criticized for his precious manners; Thomas Artus' *L'Isle des hermaphrodites* (1605) depicted Henri's effete favorites as eating with pronged forks, even though more "artichokes, asparagus, peas and beans slip between their tines" than were successfully eaten. The fork carried such a stigma that well into the seventeenth century Louis XIV preferred eating with his fingers. He was even able to eat chicken stew with his hands, according to the memoirs of Louis de Rouvroy, duc de Saint-Simon.

But the fork was too useful to be rejected forever; its use spread throughout Europe "following the path of Italian humanism, emigrating from Venice, Naples, Florence, and Rome northward to France, from which, in the late seventeenth and eighteenth centuries, they spread through the Continent, Britain, and eventually Europe's colonies." Those able to afford worked metal pieces began carrying their own knife, fork, and spoon traveling sets, though by the early eighteenth-century French aristocrats, following Versailles' practice, began keeping tableware and cutlery for their guests. Where France went, the rest of Europe followed.

Once the fork had caught on, it proliferated wildly. I understand that in America during the nineteenth century the fork became a focus of social anxiety: "a silver fork was the most ubiquitous symbol of affluence… In a nation that claimed to be a classless society, quotidian flatware had become the most significant and exquisitely calibrated marker of one's status." The grande dame of American manners, Emily Post, even went so far as to condemn the endless variations on the fork: a fork for raw oysters, for terrapin, for strawberries, for grapefruit, for fish…

Mamie gave me her own Christofle silver flatware, which is stamped with an Art Nouveau lotus pattern. It is engraved with the initials of Guy (Mamie's maiden name) and Follet (her married name), as was traditional. I use the pieces every day.

Eating with Mamie's silver, no meal is ever ordinary…

Restaurant | Famous Chef:

Christofle silverware

https://www.christofle.com/

French 75

As strange as it may sound, I only tried my first French 75 cocktail in Hong Kong. In France, you see, we rarely mix Champagne with any other ingredients (apart from Kir Royale). Only in the last few years have the French encouraged a revival of the old cocktails, classics which were invented during Prohibition: the Sazerac, Mint Julep, Daiquiri, Tom Collins, Margarita, Side Car, Manhattan, and Martini.

A French 75 is made of gin, sugar syrup, lemon juice and Champagne. It is a classic aperitif which can appeal to any palate and has a luxurious finish thanks to its champagne.

The legend goes that the cocktail was created by a WWI French-American fighter pilot, Gervais Raoul Lufbery, who served with the Escadrille Lafayette (a squadron of American volunteers who joined France before the United States officially entered the war). Lufbery became famous after dying by jumping from his burning plane. He is also remembered for creating a cocktail made with gin, Champagne, lemon juice and sugar. The idea came as he was looking to add a kick to the Champagne by adding some stronger alcohol.

The name French 75 refers the fact that Lufbery joked that the drink had a jolt as powerful as a French 75mm gun used by the French Army.

Though the Lufbery story is a romantic one, it is commonly held that Harry MacElhone, of Harry's New York Bar in Paris, made the first French 75. There is also some dispute as to whether the original version might have been made with cognac instead of gin. These days, to avoid confusion, we call the version of the cocktail made with Cognac a French 95, while one with bourbon is a French 69, and with vodka French 76... Whether the doomed hero invented the drink, or the professional bartender, everyone agrees that it was first drunk by the Lost Generation during WW1.

A mon commandement... En joue... Tirez!

Ready! Aim! Fire!

Recipe:

French 75 recipe video by Eben Freeman

http://www.epicurious.com/video/cocktails/cocktails-classics/1915458821/how-to-make-a-french-75/1915433483

Restaurant | Famous Chef:

Harry's New York Bar, Paris

http://www.harrys-bar.fr/-cocktails-.html

French Fries

French fries are julienned potatoes deep fried in oil. Though French myself, I am a little reluctant to claim the ubiquitous French fry for my country, since the Belgians are prepared to fight for the title. Etymology backs up a French origin, though, since "fries" derives from French: the past participle of *frire* ("deep fry").

The third president of the United States, Thomas Jefferson, who was a diplomatic minister to France during the late eighteenth century, and who introduced French cuisine to the newly fledged United States, very likely was responsible for bringing French fries to Washington DC from Paris. A list of recipes in Jefferson's own handwriting exists at his home in Monticello, Virginia; the list includes *pommes de terre frites à crû, en petites tranches* (potatoes, fried in deep fat while raw, first cut into small slices). Improbable, but true. What he would have made of the "Freedom Fry" controversy 200 years later is anybody's guess.

The Spanish first brought the potato ('patata') to Europe from South America (genetic testing has traced potato back to Peru, though most cultivated potatoes today come from a Chilean variant); in Spain's Basque region, potatoes were quickly adopted, becoming a preferred accompaniment for fried fish. Meanwhile we French were slow to see the culinary possibilities of the somewhat unremarkable looking tuber: the Paris Faculty of Medicine declared it edible only in 1772, after the physician Antoine Parmentier repeatedly promoted the vegetable – he threw dinner parties with potatoes as the star ingredient and went so far as to offer King Louis XVI and his wife potato blossom bouquets. Parmentier's passion for the potato lives on in the *hachis parmentier*, which is very similar to the shepherd's pie: it includes minced beef served in potato shells, drizzled with sauce lyonnaise (white wine, vinegar, and onions).

To make great French fries, use high starch russet potatoes (like the Idaho); get ones that are a little old, with wrinkled skins – this will give texture to your *frites*; fry them twice (the first at 170 C°, the second at around 190°C) – and eat them immediately when they're hot.

As the Belgians say: *Tu as la frite une fois*! (Are you full of energy?)

Recipe:	**Restaurant | Famous Chef:**
Steak Tartare & Chips	Gordon Ramsay, *A Chef for All Seasons*, p. 197

Galette des Rois & The King's Cake

Every Epiphany (6 January), the feast day that celebrates the day the Three Kings arrived to worship the infant Jesus, my father would buy a Galette des Rois. My sisters and I would eat our slices quickly, each hoping to be lucky enough to find the fève (figurine, originally 'bean', in French) hidden within the cake's delectable almond and golden pastry filling. Whoever found the trinket would be the king (or queen, as you can sometimes find two trinkets in a cake) for the day and would get to wear the gilt paper crown. Eating my slice, and hoping for the treat, is one of my oldest childhood memories.

The traditional Galette des Rois is made of puff pastry and frangipane filling made from almonds. The word *frangipane* comes from the Italian "*frangere il pane*" ("break the bread"). I love frangipane served just barely warm; I love how its almond smell fills up a room.

The Kings' Cake, however, is a brioche with candied fruits inside, akin to a panettone. The King's Cake has many names around the world, but all include the ceremonial crowning of the child as the bean king, with the bean representing the infant Jesus. But the ritual has an ancient pagan antecedent: Saturnalia. During this festival, Rome's lower classes were allowed to parody their masters, while feasting and drinking. A golden round cake representing the sun was served when the meal finished. Then as now, the king of the banquet was whoever found the bean.

Galette des Rois & The King's Cake

The "bean king," or trinket, was at some point replaced by porcelain figurines of a king, though during the French Revolution the *pâtissiers* with a view to self-preservation wisely began crafting other shapes. By the twentieth century, they were made of plastic, porcelain, or even gold, taking every conceivable form – starfish, tiny Tour Eiffels, butterflies, owls, Pierrots.

My mother herself has saved every fève she has ever found; her favourites are a delicate porcelain infant Jesus and one Louis d'Or stamped with the name of the baker's shop. One baker decided to promote his shop by placing a real Louis d'Or, (valued today at around US$2,800), inside one of the Galette des Rois: what brilliant (if rather expensive) marketing!

Gazpacho

When I lived in Spain, my fridge always had a vat of gazpacho in it; it was my favourite way to refresh myself. Some of you might think that as a Frenchman I should prefer the famous cold soup Vichysoisse (which was invented in America by a French chef) made of pureed leeks, onions, potatoes, cream and chicken stock, but I find that soup too rich and thick for my taste.

Gazpacho has the playful nickname 'liquid salad.' In the winter, it can be hot; in the summer, it's served cold. There are many regional varieties, but the most famous version comes from Andalusia, and is made with tomatoes, bell peppers, cucumbers, garlic and bread moistened with water blended with olive oil, vinegar and iced water. If you want to try a great gazpacho, I recommend to try José Andrés' restaurant Jaleo. Andrés worked with Ferran Adrià at El Bulli. I met Andres once at one of Madrid's tapas bars, Los Huevos de Lucio.

Gazpacho's origins date back to the era when Spain belonged to the Islamic world (from roughly 711 until 1212). The soup's original base was an *ajo blanco*, or garlic soup, and included garlic, almonds, bread, olive oil, vinegar and salt. Tomatoes and bell peppers were only after the Americas were discovered and colonized. Those vegetables were still left out in Juan de la Mata's mid-eighteenth-century cookbook *Arte de reposteria*.

The word gazpacho derives from an Arabic word for 'soaked bread.' Culinary historians have traced its influences back to the Roman Empire, as vinegar was a mainstay of Roman cooking; it's the vinegar that gives this soup its tang, its refreshing sharpness in the summer.

A variation of the gazpacho is *salmorejo,* which contains neither bell peppers nor cucumber, and is more viscous because it contains more bread than traditional gazpacho. For garnish, it has diced Serrano ham and diced hard-boiled eggs. *Salmorejo* is more orange than ruby red.

So, the next time you pick up a glass of gazpacho, remember: you're drinking Spain's history in a single glass – from classical antiquity (garlic and vinegar), to the medieval Islamic caliphate (almonds); to its colonial conquests (tomatoes, peppers).

Viva España!

Recipe:

Gazpacho recipe from Jose Andres

http://www.productsfromspain.net/food/alvalle-gazpacho

Restaurants | Famous Chefs:

Jose Andres group

http://thinkfoodgroup.com/

Alvalle Gazpacho

http://www.productsfromspain.net/food/alvalle-gazpacho

Grog

Grog always reminds me of my grandmother, who would administer it when I was down with flu. She promised it would cure my sore throat. Yes, my first taste of alcohol was for medicinal purposes! For those who have never had grog: it is a drink made with lemon juice, water, rum and cinnamon.

But where does its name come from?

During long sea voyages, sailors would suffer from scurvy, or vitamin C deficit – they were unable to keep perishable fresh fruits on board for their journey's duration; their meat and grain diet proved insufficient. Primates are almost the only animal unable to synthesize their own vitamin C. Guinea pigs also are unable to complete the trick.

When the British navy took Jamaica from the Spanish in 1655, rum replaced beer as the British sailors' rations. A half pint each day, as you may imagine, proved rather too much. So, Admiral Edward Vernon, or "Old Grog" – nicknamed after the wool/ silk blend grogram cloth cloak that he wore in bad weather – begun diluting his sailors' rum rations. He added water and lime juice at a 4:1 ratio, because over long sea voyages the water was brackish. The citrus' acid made stale water more palatable and the British took the nickname of "limeys" for their extensive use of the lime.

Later the British navy realized that the Admiral's sailors were much healthier than those on other ships, since the lime juice rich in Vitamin C was an excellent preventative of flu as well.

The British navy passed grog on to the American navy and to the Australians through their settlements. But you can find traces of the grog in countries such as Sweden or the Caribbean's. The word *grog* even took different meanings in countries like Australia, where grog can describe any alcoholic beverage.

Obviously, the use of grog as a remedy against the flu has disappeared, apart from in the countryside villages of France, where there is always a grand-mère to remind us that the simplest cures are often the best ones.

Merci, Petite Mamie!

Recipe:

Grog recipe
http://thinkfoodgroup.com/

Hainan Chicken

I first came across this dish in Hong Kong, where it is justly popular. I have since eaten Hainan Chicken at restaurants throughout Asia, but I believe (without prejudice!) that the Mandarin Oriental's Café Causette serves the best version anywhere. Sorry, Singapore!

Whenever I entertained friends at Hong Kong Mandarin Oriental's Clipper Lounge or in Café Causette, I recommended that they try the Hainan Chicken. It would never be so good anywhere else, I always said.

The Mandarin's Hainan Chicken was simplicity itself, all flavours intensified and harmonized: the bowl of chicken broth served with a scattering of bright red wolfberries (also known as medlars); the 'oily rice,' cooked in lemongrass, salt, chicken fat, vegetable oil and our kitchen's secret master stock; baby bok choi; and delicious Loong Kwong chicken from Wei Yang in China. On the side we served a ginger chutney, dark sweet soy and chili sauce.

The chef created this version in 2003, by adapting a Hainan dish called Wenchang Chicken. (Ironically there is no 'Hainan chicken' in Hainan. And the Singaporeans know it merely as "chicken rice.") At the Mandarin, we boiled the chicken whole, seasoning it with garlic, ginger, lemongrass, galangal and shallot.

I do not think that there is a protocol regarding the order in which you should eat different ingredients. I prefer the tender white meat (breast) to the dark (leg). I also remove the yellow skin and dip the meat either in the pureed ginger or in the sweet soy sauce. I then eat the oily rice and

Hainan Chicken

finish with the chicken broth to wash everything down.

If chicken soup ever existed as a Platonic ideal, it's this one.

Recipes:

Hainan chicken recipe from Café Causette

Restaurants | Famous Chefs:

Café Causette, Hong Kong

http://www.mandarinoriental.com/hongkong/dining/restaurants/cafe_causette/

Hamburger

A Hamburger is, of course, a citizen of Germany's northern port of Hamburg. Once upon a time, it's said, a cook from that city pan fried minced raw beef. He added condiments and sandwiched the steak between two buns to keep the grease off his hands. A classic was born. This dish travelled with the many Germans who immigrated to the New World.

In 2006, I wanted to create a true gourmet hamburger for Madrid's restaurant ESTIK, which specialized in exotic meats: we served ostrich, kudu, and crocodile. I wanted to offer the best meat available. So, we selected sirloin of Kobe beef, but as we could not obtain an import permit for Japanese *wagyu*, we sourced it from New Zealand and Australia – ESTIK was the first to import wagyu into Spain.

The chef added mâche, caramelized onions, kumato tomato (which tastes especially sweet and has a strong, crunchy skin whose colour ranges from green to a dark red colour), and a homemade brioche bun dusted with poppyseeds. Fixing the selling price at €85, I thought it would surely be the world's most expensive. I was right; at that time Daniel Boulud held the record with his *foie gras* and black truffle hamburger (€69).

The press loved the idea of our having a spat over it: two boys from Lyons go *mano a mano* over a burger. The Spanish newswires took up the story, and a Catalan radio station did live interviews with Daniel and me about our respective hamburgers. Daniel claimed that our Kobe burger was not 'real,' because the meat was not ground; I riposted that hamburger itself is no more than seared steak tartare (tenderized meat).

I lost the record, though, when Daniel created the DB Double Truffle Burger (double its predecessor's size, and with more truffles). Boulud priced this behemoth at $134.

Years later I would meet Boulud in person; he was not only the most charming and humble of chefs, but he also had a great sense of humour. I didn't remind him of the earlier *contretemps,* which was largely an invention of the press.

Today the most expensive hamburger can be found in Las Vegas, inside the Mandalay Bay Resort, at the restaurant Fleur. The Fleurburger is worth $5,000 and consists of wagyu beef, seared foie gras and black truffle.

I preferred the days when the Lyonnais were holding the record!

Recipes:

The DB "Royale" double truffle burger

http://money.cnn.com/galleries/2007/news/0710/gallery.luxury_expensive_food/index.html

Restaurants | Famous Chefs:

DB Bistro Moderne, New York

http://www.danielnyc.com/dbbistro.html

Herbs of Provence

I love the Herbs de Provence – drunk in an infusion; set out on windowsills to keep scorpions out of the house; to make the pantry fragrant. I also love these herbs sprinkled on grilled meat in a midsummer garden while crickets sing near the barbecue.

The herbs were first known for their medicinal values: oregano disinfects; rosemary aids digestion and keeps the scalp healthy; thyme is excellent for asthma; while basil relieves cramps; and sarriette is an aphrodisiac.

Herbs of Provence travel well and can be stored for years on a shelf without deteriorating. In 2003, a red label, or warranty, was first issued to certify the herbs' purity. To receive the red label, all sachets must come from Provence, and be blended according to the following ratio: 19% thyme, 26% rosemary, 3% basil, 26% oregano and 26% sarriette.

These flavours go well with grilled fish, poultry or beef. I love scattering them directly over my charcoal fire, so the aromatic smoke also flavours the meat.

But the use of the herbs of Provence as a blend can be controversial in some quarters: some inhabitants of the region will tell you that their herbs are not meant to be mixed and should be used separately. Here are a few recommendations:

Basil	Tomato / Soup
Fennel	Fish

Juniper	Game / Beef
Laurel	Fish / Beef
Rosemary	Lamb
Sage	Pork
Savory	Cheese
Thyme	Veal / Chicken

I also recommend that my readers visit l'Atelier de Jean-Luc Rabanel, an excellent restaurant in Arles, where the chef has mastered all the herbs from Provence. He grows most known varieties in his garden and has even rediscovered forgotten ones! Jean-Luc Rabanel is known as one of the first "Bio chefs" and has won two Michelin stars and a 19/20 rating from the *Gault et Millau* guide making him top 16 restaurants in France. He also created the concept of "La Cuisine du Vivant," which demands that we use all the vegetables possible: "Cultivate a hundred varieties of each vegetable to obtain an infinite palette of textures and flavours. Surprise with a rare tomato, a never before seen aubergine… and choose only the best!"

So, get out to the barbecue and try les herbs de Provence!

Restaurants | Famous Chefs:

L'Atelier de Jean-Luc Rabanel
http://www.rabanel.com/

Honeymoon

What, you may ask, does honey have to do with the tradition of newlywed couples taking a trip after the wedding ceremony?

According to Anatoly Liberman, an etymologist with Oxford University Press, the word *honeymoon* first appeared in English in 1546, when it was apparently already in common use. Love begins as honey, "but will change as the moon." In Tudor England, the verb *to honey* meant "to talk fondly, to coax." The English verb was translated into French as *lune de miel*; from French, the expression spread into Spanish and Italian.

I spent my honeymoon in Bangkok and then at the Mandarin Dhara Dhevi in Chiang Mai; the hotel is named after the goddess of enlightenment! We felt as if we had been transported to an ancient temple complex within the jungle's screen.

One of my great pleasures was eating in Chiang Mai's restaurants and from its street stalls. The region around the city, in Thailand's north, was a Burmese tributary kingdom in ancient times, when it was called Lanna. Chiang Mai's local cuisine has its own distinctive produce and cooking traditions, which I found an amazing contrast to all the spicy meals with sweet overtones that we had eaten in Bangkok. Food in Thailand's north is at times a little bitter, though still delicious. For any of my readers interested in trying the city's famous fermented noodles (*kao soi*), or its sausage, (*sai ouah*), I recommend David Thompson's *Thai Food*, which includes recipes for making them!

Thompson also describes Lanna ingredients little known in Europe and the States: *macquem*, dried berries of the prickly ash, which are spicy and carry "a delicate mandarin perfume"; base stocks made out of land crabs simmered with lemongrass until the paste becomes "thick, black and murky"; and curries and soups made with the leaves and shoots gathered from the Thai Highlands. For the adventurous, Lanna's less refined jungle food includes dishes made from deer, snakes, turtles, lizards, as well as ants and even gibbons. I gave those plates a wide berth, preferring the chicken curries and *kao soi* noodles.

Sometimes I think my divorce is due to the fact that during the years after our marriage, every time we were going on a trip, I told the hotel we were on honeymoon to get some free goodies. Don't tell the trick!

Recipes:

Chiang Mai Kao soi

Restaurants | Famous Chefs:

Thai Food, 571-2

HP Sauce

You can tell a lot about who people are by looking at the table settings where they eat. The flatware will tell you what courses will be served. Champagne flutes? A celebration. Brandy snifters with bottles of Hennessy V.S.O.P? Perhaps a Cantonese wedding. Tiny colour stickers on the wine glasses? A vertical tasting (the same wine, different vintages). HP Sauce? Then we must be in the UK.

I first came across HP sauce during my London years in the cafés the English affectionately call 'greasy spoons.' The English swear by their fry ups (toast with baked beans, grilled tomatoes and mushrooms, sausage, black pudding, and bacon) as hang-over cures. And no fry up is complete without HP Sauce. One of the most enduring of England's so-called bottled brown sauces, which are made of malt vinegar with spices and fruits, HP Sauce is used as condiment on shepherd's pie (minced lamb and mashed potatoes) or cottage pie (beef with mashed potatoes); the English also use brown sauce to correct their curries, if they come out too bitter. I myself preferred brown sauce on bacon and sausage sandwiches.

In 1875, Edwin Samson Moore founded the Midlands Vinegar Company, and began expanding his business to include sauces with exotic Asian spices. When visiting one of his debtors, a Nottingham grocer called F. G. Garton, Moore saw a basket cart with the letters HP SAUCE emblazoned on its side. When Moore asked him about the name, Garton said it was short for "Houses of Parliament," where the sauce was served in the Members' restaurant. Moore settled the debt in exchange for the name and recipe for the sauce.

HP Sauce

The Oxford Companion to Food takes a dim view of HP Sauce and its cousin brown bottled sauces: "They combine sweet, vinegary, and spicy elements, and often have a gummy texture… The labels make interesting reading for connoisseurs of food additives."

The Lea & Perrins sauce – more often called Worcestershire Sauce – is a more distinguished relation. Two nineteenth century chemists, John Lea and William Perrins, created it according to a recipe that a traveller had brought back from Bengal. The sauce consists of malt vinegar, sugar, molasses, salt, anchovies, tamarind, garlic, and onions.

Who says the British don't have their own gastronomic traditions?

Restaurants | Famous Chefs:

HP official website

http://www.hpsauce.co.uk/

Indian Tonic Water

Who would have thought that one of the most popular mixed drinks, the G + T (gin and tonic) was originally created to swallow a medicine? Ever wondered why it is called Indian, or why it glows in the shadows of a night club?

I owe this story to a friend of mine, James Riley, who recounted it as we sailed to Po Toi Island from Hong Kong's Deep-Water Bay.

Indian Tonic Water is a carbonated beverage flavoured with quinine, which is used to treat malaria. It was 'invented' by the British in India as a pleasant way of taking a daily dose of quinine to prevent malaria. The gin or vodka was added by those who still found the drink unpleasant.

The water's bitter taste comes from the quinine, which was added in even higher measures under the British Raj. It is also due to the presence of the quinine that the beverage fluoresces under ultraviolet light, since quinine will fluoresce even in direct sunlight.

Quinine is also used in the traditional Vesper Martini, which includes gin, vodka and Kina Lillet, an aperitif created in the late nineteenth century. Kina Lillet came from Bordeaux; discontinued in 1986, it was made from wine, quinine and a mix of fruit liqueurs. Today there are new versions called Lillet Blanc and Lillet Rouge. The word Kina comes from quinine harvested from the *cinchona* tree, which grows throughout South America.

The Vesper Martini first appeared at Boodles, a club Ian Flemings used to frequent. He then used it in his first James Bond novel, *Casino*

Royale. Bond says: "Shake until ice cold and serve in a deep Champagne goblet with a large thin slice of lemon peel."

I have never been a huge fan of Indian tonic water, and perhaps for that reason I never drink Gin + Tonic. Nowadays bartenders around the world who are always trying to offer the best quality drinks make their own tonic water by boiling cinchona bark (containing quinine) as a tea, adding citrus and agave nectar as a sweetener and then carbonate the liquid using a soda charger.

So, it's not just a spoonful of sugar that makes the medicine go down.

Recipe:

Hendrick's Gin & Tonic

http://www.hendricksgin.com/#/us

John Dory

John Dory is a fish with a fascinating shape and an almost comically ferocious face, whose body is so thin that it is filleted like a flat fish. Found mainly in the Mediterranean, it has been caught as far north as Norway, and has relatives in Australian and north-western Pacific waters.

The John Dory is valued as a high-quality fish for its fine but meaty texture, its low-fat content, and for its subtle but delicious flavours. The fish is usually prepared by grilling, sautéing or poaching; it is popular with chefs because it can be combined with a wide variety of ingredients. Even its bones are useful: they make excellent fish stock.

The name was probably taken from a sixteenth century Cornish folksong about a French pirate whose ship was called the *John Dory*:

> '*Who ho, who ho, a goodly ship I do see;*
> *I trow it to be John Dory, o.*'

'Dory' is a corruption of the French word for gilt ('dorée').

The same fish is known to the French, Italians and Spanish as Saint Peter, in reference to the black mark ringed with gold on each flank. These dark shapes supposedly would flash the Evil Eye at approaching dangers. A legend says that the marks represent the place where Saint Peter clasped the fish, following Jesus' prophecy that he would catch a fish that carried a silver coin in its mouth; that coin, Jesus told Peter, should be given to the temple tax collectors.

When I worked at the Bluebird Restaurant in the King's Road, we used John Dory for Fish and Chips. We considered it a provocative choice, to use such a luxurious fish (rather than plaice, whiting, or haddock) for a dish that is usually associated with greasy newspapers and take-away shops. But our customers loved it.

And they're always right.

Recipes:

John Dory recipe by Pierre Gagnaire

http://www.forbes.com/2010/06/10/pierre-gagnaire-twist-lifestyle-food-travels-in-taste.html

Restaurants | Famous Chefs:

Bluebird restaurant, London

http://www.danddlondon.com/restaurants/bluebird/home

Karkade

Karkady is the Arabic name for hibiscus tea, a herbal drink rich in vitamin C, and made from infusions of the hibiscus flower, *hibiscus sabdariffa*. It is drunk both hot and cold (when it is known as *einab*); whatever its temperature, it has a beautiful red tint. The Egyptians knew it as 'the jewel-red brew.'

In the mid-1990s, I lived in Egypt, teaching French at the Hotel School of Luxor, just behind the great temple. I also ran a project for the French ambassador, Patrick Leclercq, and Egypt's First Lady, Suzanne Mubarak, to start a public kindergarten that taught French and Arabic. The school opened with three classes and ninety children.

I will never forget watching the sunset from the Sofitel Winter Palace's terrace. This hotel, then run by my friend Denis de Schrevel, was built in 1886 on the Nile's banks. It was here that Howard Carter stayed when he found the Tutankhamun's tomb in 1922; it was here that Agatha Christie wrote *Death on the Nile* in 1933. The palace has a beautiful garden of bougainvillea and clipped palm trees. As the sun disappeared from the horizon, I was never without a cold glass of *einab*. Most of Egypt's supply comes from hibiscus plantations that cluster throughout the arid burning land near the oasis of Fayoum in Upper Egypt, although some karcady is produced along the Nile delta itself.

Karcady can also be found in South America, where it is called *Agua de Flor de Jamaica* (Jamaican flower water), and is drunk chilled with ginger, sugar and rum. In Asia it is often called roselle, and drunk cold.

Recently an American study proved that the antioxidants contained in karcady are excellent remedies for hypertension. So ancient Egyptians were advanced not only in agriculture, architecture and medicine by several thousand years, but also in energy drinks!

If you don't believe me, try *karcade* yourself!

Recipes:

Karkade recipe

http://recipes.wikia.com/wiki/Karkade_(Iced_Hibiscus_Drink)

Restaurants | Famous Chefs:

The Winter Palace, Luxor

http://www.sofitel.com/gb/hotel-1661-sofitel-winter-palace-luxor/index.shtml

Kellogg's / Liebig - The Physicians

There are many physicians who have contributed to contemporary health food; these include Justus von Liebig and John Kellogg.

As a child I always ate cornflakes for breakfast before school. I loved the puzzles, stories and jokes on the Kellogg's box, and the little prizes hidden among the cereal.

As for von Liebig – his name brings back images of the small beef bouillon cubes my grandmother sometimes used when she was in a hurry to cook pasta or soups. This Liebig cube was named after its parent company, the Liebig Extract of Meat Company (now Oxo). The Liebig cube, once called Extractum carnis Liebig, (or ersatz meat), is produced using beef carcasses at a ratio of 3kg of meat for each 100g of extract.

Baron von Liebig was a German chemist who became known as the father of the fertilizer industry following his discovery of nitrogen as a vital nutrient for growing plants. Liebig's company was the first sponsor of the Olympic Games in 1908, providing athletes with energy drinks that promised to increase their stamina and strengthen their muscles.

Here's a recipe to remember : take one beef oxo cube, add vodka, Tabasco, Worcestershire sauce, salt and pepper: you have got yourself a cocktail called Bull Shot! It's a drink that I'm very fond of, and I can't think why the company left it out of the 1893 *Liebig's Practical Cookery Book*.

Kellogg's / Liebig - The Physicians

Kellogg, meanwhile, developed a number of items that he quaintly referred to as 'hygienic comestibles' for the benefit of his patients. These included peanut butter, and a double-baked breadcrumb cereal that he called 'Granola.'

But Kellogg's most famous creation is cooked wheat flakes, which he wanted his patients to eat as a dry snack. His recalcitrant invalids promptly made the horse feed more palatable by adding milk and sugar to the flakes and substituting the sweeter corn flake for the more austere wheat.

John Kellogg and his brother Will actually fell out over whether the flakes should be sweetened; unable to reconcile, they broke up their company, Sanitas Food. Will then started his own company (which had the formidable name, Battle Creek Toasted Corn Flake Company – later Kellogg's) while John countered with the Battle Creek Food Company to develop America's rather less promising market for soy products. Meanwhile, in Switzerland, Max Bircher-Benner, another doctor, was developing muesli. Bircher-Benner is remembered as one of the first nutritionists who promoted a lifestyle based on harmony between people and nature.

At breakfast, I drink a green juice and have some Greek yoghurt with granola and berries!

Recipes:

Antoine's Bull Shot recipe

Restaurants | Famous Chefs:

Oxo Tower restaurant, London
http://www.harveynichols.com/output/Page128.asp

Kir

Kir was probably the first cocktail I enjoyed as a child. It originated in Burgundy near my hometown Lyons and is made with white wine mixed with crème de cassis (blackcurrant liqueur), which children love. And again, it was Mamie who gave me my first Kir.

Crème de cassis is a blood-red, sweet liqueur made with blackcurrants crushed in refined alcohol then with some sugar added. It is believed that the popularity of this somewhat old-fashioned drink rose again after WWII, due to a surplus of white Burgundy.

Kir was first called *blanc-cass*, which literally means 'broken white.' The white wine used for this drink is traditionally made from the *Aligoté* grape. Felix Kir, mayor of Dijon in the 1950s, liked to add the crème de cassis from Dijon to the Bourgogne Aligoté wine, which he found too acidic. Kir always served the *Blanc-cass* at parties held in the city hall to promote two products of the region. The drink thus took the name of the mayor.

Variations include the famous Kir Royale, which is served as an aperitif at gala dinners; Kir Royale is made with Champagne and crème de cassis. Another version, which Mamie often made, is the Communard, which marries the crème de cassis to red wine. The word 'Communard' refers to the massacres that occurred in 1871 when 20,000 communards (members of the Paris Commune created after the Franco-Prussian war) were killed in skirmishes with the French army.

At the Soneva Fushi, in the Maldives' Baa Atoll, we organize cocktails on a sandbank in the middle of the Indian Ocean for the resort's guests. It is here that I most enjoy my Kir: watching the sunset with our guests and colleagues in paradise.

Santé, Petite Mamie!

Restaurants | Famous Chefs:

Bourgogne Aligote, Olivier Leflaive

http://www.olivier-leflaive.com/beaune-blanc.php3?id_article=361

The Knife

As a very small boy, I found it extremely difficult to use a knife. Perhaps it was the weight of the blade's handle, or maybe I just had to develop the necessary finesse, but it took me a while before I could slice meat myself.

I learned about knives from Mamie: she used her Savoyard Opinel knife for almost everything and loved how it balanced in her hand. My grandfather Pape had his own personal knife, which he brought to the table and took with him everywhere.

My first knife was an Opinel, which I received when I was a Boy Scout. Then at twelve, I was given a Victorinox, the iconic Swiss Army knife – red, with a little white cross on it. The knife wasn't just a knife; it had many functions: scissors, corkscrew, toothpick, screwdriver, twizzle, and even compass. When I was seventeen, I was given a hunting knife, a Herbetz folding blade, from my aunt and uncle's hunting shop Plume & Poil (Feather & Hide). I was extremely proud of that knife. Its edge was incredibly sharp – it could flense an animal of its skin, although let me assure you that I never did anything more bloodthirsty with it than whittle sticks.

Particularly in France, Germany, and England, the knife has long evoked social status: "Even today, particularly in English and American homes, the head of the family is still expected to carve the holiday roast with well-heeled dignity and grace, symbolically re-enacting the rights of the lord of the manor."

Across the Channel, the protocols for using knives became more refined during the Enlightenment: in 1637, Armand du Plessis (best known to history and readers of *The Three Musketeers* as Cardinal Richelieu) ordered that the points of all his dining knives be filed down, apparently in a fit of understandable disgust after watching his guests floss their teeth with their own daggers.

As any *savoir vivre* book advises, it is déclassé to cut salad with your knife. This stricture dates from the time when tableware was sterling silver, which vinaigrette can ruin.

On a sentimental note, you may have heard that when giving a knife as a present, you must receive a token coin in return, lest the blade sever your friendship… Or, as we say in France: *"Celui qui estrine sa dame par amour, le jour de l'an, de couteau, sachez que leur amour refroidira…"*

Restaurants | Famous Chefs:

Opinel
http://www.opinel.com

Kosher

One of my closest friends at the École Hotelière de Lausanne, Alexandre Izralewicz, introduced me to *kashrut,* the Jewish dietary laws, during our student days. Alexandre then owned the great modern bistro Balthazar in Paris, which itself is not kosher; one of his signature dishes calls for escargots!

Kashrut stipulations are complex and sometimes counterintuitive. A ban on boiling a kid in its mother's milk (Exodus 23:19) is understood to forbid combining dairy products and meat in the same meal. Kosher kitchens keep separate cooking utensils, plates and cutlery for meat and dairy meals to ensure there is no cross-contamination; in larger catering establishments this can even extend to having separate kitchens.

On clean and unclean food, a chef is warned to distinguish "between the clean beast and the unclean, and between the unclean bird and the clean…" (Leviticus 20: 24-25). The list that follows includes fish; anything living in water is considered clean, so long as it has both fins and scales (shellfish and molluscs are thus forbidden). Most domestic fowl are clean; ostriches, pelicans, storks and birds of prey are not, nor (as you might expect) are reptiles. Leviticus even stipulates certain insects to be fit for consumption, but most are not, meaning that all produce must be carefully checked for bugs.

On land, all kosher animals must both have cloven hooves and chew their cud. Cows, sheep and goats are acceptable, whereas camels, rabbits and pigs, which only meet one of these criteria, are not. Venison can be kosher, but only if it is slaughtered by the method known as *shechitah*. As deer are generally shot in the open field, it is rarely available outside areas with large Jewish communities, but in the early twentieth century *shochets* (ritual slaughterers) would visit the Rothschild estate in England and slaughter deer for the British market.

The *shechitah* method of slaughter stems from a law forbidding eating flesh with its 'life,' or blood. (Genesis 9:3-4). According to Hebrew tradition, animals have souls, and murder was forbidden : meat-eating could be rationalized only if the food animal's life was returned directly to God as a blood libation. Animals are slaughtered via a single cut to the throat, severing the main arteries to drain the blood from the carcass. The raw meat is then salted and inspected to ensure it is healthy and unblemished.

Nowadays you can even drink Kosher Coca-Cola!

Restaurants | Famous Chefs:

Balthazar restaurant, Paris

http://restaurant-balthazar.fr/

Kugelhopf

I am sure most of my readers will never have heard of the kugelhopf. I myself was ignorant of it before meeting Chef Lichtenauer at Lausanne. Though he lives in Switzerland, Lichtenauer has remained an Alsatian at heart, and is passionate about his region's food. Thanks to him, I learnt how to make a kugelhopf.

The kugelhopf is a yeast cake made of flour, eggs, butter and sugar; it is a cousin to the brioche, baba and savarin. It contains raisins and sometimes lemon peel. A finished Kugelhopf is dusted with a snowfall of icing sugar before being served.

But most characteristic of the kugelhopf is its shape: a tall ring with a large circular hole in the middle. The mould in which it is baked is round and deep, with a central funnel, and fluted with decorative swirls which you cannot miss.

The word kugelhopf comes from the German *Kugel* ('a ball' or 'round'), in reference to its shape. Ashkenazi Jews have a similar cake, known as the *kugel.* The Kugelhopf originated in the countries of central Europe: Germany, Austria, Switzerland, Hungary, Croatia. In English, the cake's baking pan is called a 'Turk's head mould,' or bundt pan. In Alsace kugelhopf is so popular that the town of Ribeauville celebrates a fête in its honour every June. In *The Lutèce Cookbook,* Andre Soltner relates the story that the Three Kings were traveling from Bethlehem back to Cologne, and decided to break their journey at the village of Ribeauville. A pastry chef called Kugel received them; to thank him, they created a cake in the shape of a turban and named it after their host.

I recommend kugelhopf for breakfast. Dip a slice in tea or coffee so the spongy texture can soak up the liquid.

How could I forget my first cake?

Recipe:

Kugelhopf recipe

http://www.epicurious.com/recipes/food/views/Kugelhopf-106380

LAGUIOLE

I recently ordered some bespoke Laguiole knives with oak handles; the blades are engraved with the restaurant's name, the Mandarin Oriental's Krug Room. I myself own a Laguiole corkscrew that was given to me by Spanish friends, Rafael & Paz de la Vega, after a great holiday when I showed them the wonders of Provence. They had it inscribed *La Panda de la Provenza*: the Provence Gang.

The word Laguiole – which signifies both a knife and a village in France's Aubrac – comes from La Gleisola, the little chapel at the village's heart. This region is sparsely populated and has more cattle (the famous Aubrac beef) than people. The village's fame comes from its eponymous knives, which have been crafted there since 1829, when Jean Pierre Calmels created the first one. The blade's design combines the Catalan *navaja* switchblade with the local shepherds' knife, the *capuchadou*, which has a fixed blade.

A Laguiole blade's handle is made either of cattle horn, or of ordinary French woods (beech and juniper), or exotic woods like ebony, olive, and snakewood. Incised with grooves, each knife also has an insect at the top, (whether a fly or a bee is a matter of contention), perhaps in recognition of *la mouche*, the 'catch' that folded up the earliest Laguiole knives. Years ago, such knives were given as coming of age presents to adolescents.

In 2000 I visited Laguiole on a pilgrimage to eat at Michel Bras, the restaurant named after its chef. Bras is famous for his wildly creative use of local flora; he uses between 250-350 herbs, many forgotten in our era of international, globalized cuisine: they have names like meadowsweet, valerian phu, baldmoney and *cistre*, which is the restaurant's emblem. You will find such ingredients nowhere else.

Éric Raffy's architecture, with its basalts, schists, granites and slates, fits in seamlessly with the Aubrac landscape. Bras complements the sleek modernity of Raffy's design with several homely touches, including Laguiole knives, which Christian Poumeyrol redesigned for Bras. This knife stays on the table throughout the meal; it is not replaced between courses.

In keeping with his restaurant's blend of the modern and the traditional, when Bras chose to put his name on a line of knives (six for the kitchen, and one steak), Bras chose the Japanese company Kai to craft them – though the brand name still reads "La Gliole, France."

Titanium coated stainless steel, and a fourteenth century shepherd's knife, in harmony.

Recipe

Michel Bras' Gargouille

Restaurants | Famous Chefs:

Michel Bras

LAUREATE

Thanks to the Provençal cuisine I love, I have chanced on the etymology of some amazing words. Here I will explain the relation between *laureate*, the title used for Nobel Prize winners, and the herb laurel, whose leaves are used in Provençal beef stews and soups.

In Greek mythology, Apollo (the god of music) unwisely insulted Eros (the god of love) by laughing at him for messing around with bows and arrows rather than heavier artillery. Furious, Eros grabbed two arrows, one of gold and one of lead; he pierced Apollo with the golden arrow (to inspire love) and then shot the lovely nymph Daphne with the leaden one (to inspire loathing). Apollo chased Daphne; she prayed to her father, a river god, asking that he help her escape. Daphne's obliging father turned her into a laurel tree… that's one way of avoiding a bad date. Disappointed but undeterred, Apollo made the laurel his own emblem: a crown for victors, for poets and athletes alike.

For the Romans, the laurel was synonymous with glory. They crowned statues of Hercules, Bacchus, and Apollo with laurel wreaths, and planted avenues of laurel trees before the emperor's palace on the Flaminian Way. After a victory, messengers would transmit a letter to Rome with a laurel branch: hence the expression, *litterae laureate*. During diploma ceremonies, today's laureates are crowned with laurel and its bays (*bacca laureate*) in Latin; the word *baccalaureat* is used in many languages.

Nobel Prize winners are also called 'laureates.' While living in Sweden, I learned that Alfred Nobel was the Swedish chemist who invented dynamite. To preserve his name for posterity, he decided to use his fortune to create a series of prizes that would recognize the best minds in different fields: chemistry, medicine, literature, physics, and peacemaking. An urban legend holds that there is no prize for mathematics because Nobel's mistress was having an affair with a mathematician…

…To the victor goes the spoils.

Restaurants | Famous Chefs:

Nobel Foundation

http://nobelprize.org/

Lavender, Rosemary, Tarragon, Sage & Basil

I love herbs, which is one of the many reasons I love Provence, which abounds in them. The following herbs don't just taste great; they have medicinal benefits, too.

Lavender

The word lavender comes from the Italian *lavanda* ("to wash"). Along with thyme, rosemary, and laurel, this plant was sewn into masks worn by doctors as they worked to counter the bubonic plague that ravaged Europe during the fourteenth century.

Rosemary

The word derives from the Latin *rosmarinus* ("dew of the sea"). In ancient Egypt, this herb symbolized immortality, whereas the Romans used it to make crowns for newlywed couples.

Tarragon

The word comes from the Arabic *tarkhum* ("little dragon"). This plant both aided digestion and was thought to have antiseptic properties that would purify the air.

Sage

It derives from the Latin *salvare* ("to heal"). A medieval legend had the Virgin Mary hide Jesus in a sage plant when King Herod sent soldiers to kill all newborn boys.

BASIL

This word derives from the Greek word for 'royal.' According to legend, Alexander the Great's men brought this plant back from India. Hindu tradition has it that a woman called Vrindra threw herself onto her dead husband's funeral pyre and was burned alive. The gods commemorated this act by turning her charred hair into a sweet-smelling plant named *tulsi*, or basil. There are over 400 varieties of basil, each with its own distinct flavour...

In my kitchen, one necessity is the *bouquet garni* (garnished bouquet) made of herbs bundled together with twine and used for soups, stocks and stews like beef bourguignon, veal blanquette, bouillabaisse, or *pot au feu*. The bouquet garni is normally composed of the following herbs: thyme, bay leaf, parsley, basil, rosemary, tarragon and vegetables.

Other famous herb mixtures are Herbs de Provence, *Ras el hanout*, curry powder, harissa...

Recipe:

Blanquette de veau recipe

http://www.epicurious.com/recipes/food/views/Cafe-Bouluds-Blanquette-de-veau-103000

Le Creuset / Staub

Many of my earliest childhood memories are of my grandmother's kitchen: Mamie cooking beef *bourguignon*, *cassoulet*, or *blanquette de veau* in her Le Creuset cocotte, an orange enamelled cast iron casserole. My grandmother loved her cocotte because it was beautifully crafted, and not only retained heat but distributed it evenly, making it the perfect receptacle for cooking stews.

Le Creuset was founded in 1925 by Armand Desaegher and Octave Aubecq: both were Belgians working in Picardy. Today Le Creuset products are among France's most popular international brands: the company's contemporary range includes the cocotte, fondue kit, jam pot, Tatin dish, and the Mario Batali risotto pot. The original colour of Le Creuset cookware was a famous shade of orange. After WW2, however, the company began experimenting with a variety of colours; 'cassis' is the most recent. Le Creuset has also worked with avant-garde designers to launch new products, including the Coquelle (by Raymond Loewy), a revamped cocotte with distinctively different handles (by Enzo Mari), and the range Futura (by J.L. Barrault).

But the culinary industry is divided between devotees of Le Creuset, and others who support Staub. (Staub's advocates include Thomas Keller, Paul Bocuse, and Joël Robuchon.) Chefs claim that Staub cookware retains heat better and distributes it more evenly than its rivals' cookware, which gives food a more consistent texture and taste.

Staub dates from 1892 as a store, when it was founded by Auguste

Waldner; it was only in 1974 that Waldner's grandson, Francis Staub, purchased a cast-iron factory and developed a cookware line.

The main difference between the two companies' products is that Staub cast iron is coated with black matte enamel, making it indestructible and resistant to scratching and chips. Those chefs who use it also claim that it lasts longer and has a more user-friendly lid. Staub even claims that "its design is so technically advanced that it actually helps to enhance the flavours of the dish." The proof is in the eating, as the English say.

But as a Frenchman, I prefer not to take sides, but to own both in my kitchen! My heart tends to go for Le Creuset because of its connection with my grandmother, whereas my professional mind favours Staub for its stylish appearance, which allows the cocotte to be brought from the oven to the table.

Funny enough, there is a Le Creuset shop on Ledbury avenue around the corner of where I live in Notting Hill.

Restaurants | Famous Chefs:

Le Creuset
http://www.lecreuset.com/
Staub
http://www.staubusa.com/

Lord & Lady

Once again, my readers may be wondering what place this entry has in a book about the history of famous dishes or drinks; as usual the answer is, more than you might think!

'Lord' is a title which referred to a prince or a feudal superior; even today in the United Kingdom it is still linked with the peerage. There are five ranks of peer: duke, marquis, earl, viscount and baron. The title Lord is mainly used for the barons, although marquis, earls and viscounts may also be addressed as 'lord' – though not a duke, who would be called 'Your Grace.'

According to Reay Tannahill's *Food in History*, the word 'lord' comes from the Old English *hlaford* ('keeper of the bread'), therefore master of the household, since bread in medieval times was considered as a luxury.

The word 'lady' comes from the Old English *hlaefdigge* ('kneader of the dough'). It seems that the Old English word for servant means "bread eater"!

As a boy, I habitually sneaked out of bed to filch a bit of *couronne* (bread shaped like a crown) from our larder. I would first eat the white airy dough, saving the dark brown crust for last. My father would drive far out of the way so he could get the best bread in the neighbourhood, which was from a *boulangerie* near the village of Francheville.

In Provence, breakfast is incomplete without a fresh *ficelle*, a slender flute which weighs half a baguette. You would normally slice it in half lengthwise to make *tartines* for fresh butter and homemade jam.

Dear Lord, as the keeper of the bread, may Thou bring it to our table every day!

Recipe:

Lidia Melon's bruschetta recipe

Macaroons

The macaroon, though small, has had an outsize effect on my life. Thanks to this little cake, I won over my ex-wife Lidia. We had known each other for only a short while when I had to leave on a trip to Paris; on my return, I brought her a box of macaroons from the famous confectioner Ladurée, and she was smitten. You will not be surprised if I tell you that our wedding cake was a macaroon pyramid. Not sure it brought me luck as we split 6 years later!!!!

The macaroon (*macaron* in French) is a type of meringue made from ground almonds, sugar and egg whites. It should be crispy on the outside and soft in the centre. The word comes from the Italian *maccarone*, from *ammacare* ('to crush'). The first macaroons were derived from Italy's amaretti or coconut macaroons.

Ladurée created the macaroon (*macaron* in French) as we now know it. It was the founder's second cousin, Pierre Desfontaines, who in the early twentieth century had the inspired idea of joining two macaroon shells with a ganache filling. After cooking, the little cakes must rest for two days, while texture and flavour come into perfect balance. Ladurée's permanent collection is made up of thirteen flavours, among them lemon, pistachio, lavender, and chocolate. Ladurée also sells a product list that changes with the seasons.

Today Ladurée stands for both tradition and contemporary elegance. The original shop opened in 1862 on Rue Royale; its décor – chubby cherubs dressed as pastry cooks – is famous. Each time I visit Paris, I stop by Ladurée, even though there's always a 45-minute queue to reach the pastry counter!

Yet while Ladurée's classical school of macaroons is thriving, the little meringue also has its postmodern interpretation. Pierre Hermé, one of the world's best pastry chefs – he's been called 'the Picasso of Pastry' – has reinterpreted the macaroon in weird and wonderful flavours: olive oil, foie gras, truffle… Some of my favourites have beautiful names: the Arabesque (apricot & pistachio), Mogador (milk chocolate & passionfruit), and Fragola (strawberry & balsamic vinegar).

I have not eaten any macaroon since my divorce – just kidding!

Recipes:

Pierre Hermé salted caramel macaron recipe
http://he-eats.com/2009/08/24/pierre-hermes-salted-caramel-macarons/

Restaurants | Famous Chefs:

Ladurée Paris
http://www.laduree.fr/index_en.htm

Madeleine

The madeleine is a famous sponge cake shaped like a scallop shell. The cake comes from Commercy, a district in northern France's Loire Valley. Marcel Proust made his *petites madeleines* famous in this passage of *Remembrance of Things Past*: "No sooner had the warm liquid mixed with the crumbs touched my palate than a shudder ran through me and I stopped, intent upon the extraordinary thing that was happening to me. An exquisite pleasure had invaded my senses, something isolated, detached, with no suggestion of its origin…" The best madeleine that I have ever had was in Lyons' La Minaudière Patisserie; when warm, it would melt in my mouth!

The madeleine first attracted attention during the seventeenth century when it was invented by Madeleine Paulmier, maid to the Marquise Perrotin de Baumont. Stanislas Leszczynski, deposed King of Poland, (see *Baba*) was holding a banquet at the chateau de Commercy, when the chef walked out before dessert had been served; or, if you believe the story, before it was even made. Madeleine then stepped into the breach, baking a recipe of her grandmother's. In gratitude, Stanislas named the cake after her; her fame became the town of Commercy's own.

Another legend has it that a young girl, while traveling on the Saint James pilgrimage to Santiago de Compostela in Spain, would offer her fellow pilgrims' little cakes that she had baked in scallop shells, which is the emblem of Saint James. Pilgrims themselves would carry scallop shells around their necks and would beg for food and drinks in a donation limited to the amount the shell could hold. The scallop shell thus became the emblem of the entire pilgrims' Way of St James, which runs from France to Santiago de Compostela in Spain. It is a journey that I would like to undertake one day.

According to legend, the body of Saint James, who had been decapitated in Palestine, were brought to Spain by boat. The craft sank off the Galician coast; St. James' remains were found on the beach, encrusted with scallops. St. James' tomb was then discovered by a hermit who said that he had a dream about the saint, and was guided to the site by a star, hence the name Compostela (*Campus Stellae* 'star field').

But it's also possible that the scallop shell is linked to ancient pageant rites of the Basque goddess Mari, and that St. James' Way was a route that her followers took to worship her.

Which do you prefer, the Saint, or Venus on the Half-Shell?

Recipes:

Almond Madeleine recipe

http://www.cooks.com/rec/view/0,166,134178-248193,00.html

Restaurants | Famous Chefs:

La Minaudière, Lyons

http://maps.google.com/maps/place?client=safari&rls=en&oe=UTF-8&um=1&ie=UTF-8&q=la+Minaudiere+lyon&fb=1&hq=la+Minaudiere&hnear=Lyon,+France&cid=17840442221136339777

Melon

With a name like mine, you can imagine how I suffered at a young age from my schoolmates' jokes. That is the reason I came up with the following story about my family, which has the additional virtue of possibly being true!

My ancestors were Florentine architects who first immigrated to France from Italy in the sixteenth century. The Melons – then calling themselves Meloni – helped build what is now known as Le Vieux Lyon, Old Lyons. Many are interred at the church of Notre-Dame de Compassion at Corbelin, a village near Lyons.

Like our family, the melon (*cucumis melo* to botanists) is a wanderer: it originated in Africa. In the Bible, the melon appears among the fruits the Israelites ate in Egypt. The Greek philosophers described it as an apple cooked by the sun (*melopepon*). French melon varietals grow from a breed that came from Armenia. King Charles VIII brought the first back after his 1494-95 expedition to Italy, where the fruit was cultivated near Cantalupo, the papal residence near Rome: hence 'cantaloupe.'

You judge a good melon by its weight, its fragrance, and by its tail. You should choose a heavy, fragrant one whose tail that should come off easily (a sign of ripeness). One market producer advised me to look at the sex of the melon, as female melons taste better. A large ring at the base identifies a female.

I love eating cantaloupe with Parma ham, though it's also good on its own with a little Port poured in its centre. In our family, we always eat cantaloupe as a starter, though many people serve it as dessert after a meal.

As for watermelon, I recommend blending it into a gazpacho, sprinkling in a little sugar and mint leaves; then passing the mixture through a sieve. Adding vodka makes for another great recipe: cut a hole in the top of the watermelon, use a funnel to pour vodka inside; keep pouring until the watermelon won't absorb more liquid; and then slice it and serve cold.

Melon regards…

Recipes:

Hamburger with melon recipe

http://www.restaurant-prevot.com/fr/les-menus/10/melon-et-2010/

Restaurants | Famous Chefs:

Restaurant Prevot, Cavaillon

http://www.restaurant-prevot.com/fr/

Mère Brazier

The Mères lyonnaises originally were house cooks for Lyons' great families: the Berliets, the Tassanari, the Eymards. By the late nineteenth century, the women who would become les Mères were striking out on their own and setting up little restaurants.

The most famous Mères are la Mère Blanc, la Mère Filloux, la Mère Poupon, la Mère Lea, and la grande Marcelle; but the most celebrated of all was la Mère Brazier. These women become so revered that in 1935 the food critic Curnonsky (Maurice Edmond Sailland) declared Lyons to be France's Capital of Gastronomy.

I think my admiration for La Mère Brazier comes in part from the many resemblances with Mamie, who was also born in Bresse; like my grandmother, La Mère Brazier had great respect and intimate knowledge of the products of our region. Paul Bocuse completed his apprenticeship with her in 1945: she was an excellent teacher as well as a cook.

La Mère Brazier was the first ever chef to receive three Michelin stars for her two restaurants, the first for her bistro on 12 rue Royale, and the second for her countryside house and restaurant outside Lyons in 1933. Today, almost 70 years later, only four other chefs have won such high recognition: Alain Ducasse (1998), Marc Veyrat (2001), Thomas Keller (2006) and Pierre Gagnaire (2019).

Though I never knew Eugénie Brazier herself, I had great respect and affection for her granddaughter Jacotte, who like me is an alumna of Lausanne. Jacotte ran the restaurant at 12 rue Royale for thirty years.

Closed from 2004 until 2008, that restaurant has reopened with Matthieu Viannay as its chef; he has stayed true to Eugenie Brazier's vision, while also introducing his own modern but classical dishes. He also kept the most famous of La Mère Brazier's dishes: an artichoke salad with foie gras, *poularde demi-deuil* (poached chicken with black truffles under the skin), and *quenelle de brochet* (a mixture of creamed pike fish) with sauce Nantua (crayfish sauce).

Let no one say that only men are good chefs! *Cherchez la femme!*

Recipes:

Poularde de Bresse demi-deuil recipe

http://www.viamichelin.fr/tpl/mag6/art200902/htm/gastro-recette-mythique.htm

Pike quenelle Nantua sauce

http://www.nytimes.com/1991/08/04/travel/fare-of-the-country-delicate-pike-quenelles-a-lyons-tradition.html?pagewanted=2

Restaurant | Famous Chef:

La Mère Brazier, Lyon

http://www.lamerebrazier.fr/

MOF

I began hearing the term 'MOF' during my earliest days in the hospitality industry, especially in the kitchens. A chef or craftsman who had earned an MOF was spoken in tones of awe bordering on reverence: so, few people ever receive it. The prize has been awarded every three years since 1923; but to date, not even 10,000 have been granted the right to wear the distinctive 'bleu, blanc, rouge' on their collars.

The reader has probably guessed that MOF does not refer to the Ministry of Finance, Meta-Object Facility or even Microsoft Operations Framework.

The term MOF, meaning Meilleur Ouvrier de France, "One of the best workers of France" is awarded every four years to the best craftsmen in a given field – there are over 200 categories, from jewellery to glass-making. In the culinary industry, a MOF recognizes artisanal bakers, butchers, charcuterie-traiteurs, the creators of *gateaux*, cheese, chocolate, ice creams and sorbets, pastry makers, sommeliers, and those who serve in restaurants: but the highest profile, the most famous category, is for cuisine.

Each chef who enters the *cuisine* competition has only limited time (five hours) to create three dishes which must attain perfection, or the nearest earthly equivalent. A panel of judges observes the competitor's agility, *savoir-faire*, technique, and interpretation of tradition. The last edition was in November 2018 with 28 applicants of which only 2 were women and only 7 received the recognition.

3 Michelin star Chef Marcon, from Le Clos des Cîmes restaurant,

failed to pass MOF three times. He insists, however, that the attempts were invaluable learning experiences.

The competition requires months of preparation, and only chefs who have become experts in their craft will obtain the award, which is given by the French President during a formal ceremony at l'Elysée.

Some MOF winners are Paul Bocuse (Monsieur Paul to those who know him), and Roger Vergé, one of the most important chefs in modern French gastronomy. Roger Vergé obtained 3 Michelin stars in 1974 for his restaurant Le Moulin de Mougins near Cannes on the French Riviera. I met him when he came to L'Alcazar in Paris, the restaurant I opened for Sir Terence Conran. He was with his business partners Paul Bocuse and the famous pastry chef Gaston Lenôtre.

If I may say, the MOF are La Crème de la Crème des Fourneaux.

Recipes:

Valerie Giscard d'Estaing Soup (soupe VGE)

Restaurants | Famous Chefs:

http://www.theworldwidegourmet.com/recipes/black-truffle-soup-elysee/

Mortadella

My understanding of Italian food began when I worked as a trainee waiter in La Villa Castagnola Hotel in Lugano, Switzerland's Italian canton. Later my knowledge was further developed thanks to one of the world's most famous epicureans, Antonio Carluccio, whom I worked with in his London restaurant Neal Street.

I was always curious to understand the meaning of the word mortadella. A large pink pork sausage made with minced pork, 15% white pork fat, mortadella is flavoured with peppercorns, nutmeg, coriander, myrtle berries and pistachios or olives.

Mortadella has its origins in Bologna, a city renowned for its excellent food since the Middle Ages. There are two possibilities for the origin of its name. The first theory claims that mortadella derives from the Italian word *mortaio*, after the mortar used to ground the pork filling into a paste. The second version traces the word back to the Latin *farcimem murtatum*, which means "sausage seasoned with myrtle berries."

I have many fond memories of the entrance to Neal Street, with its beautiful red Berkel slicing machine; that machine often held mortadella, which was served to guests as an amuse-bouche.

Be sure not to confuse mortadella with salami, which comes from Piedmonte in north-western Italy; salami is made not only with pork but also from chopped beef, venison, turkey and – at times – even horsemeat. Additional ingredients include salt, vinegar, garlic, white pepper, wine, herbs and minced fat. Mortadella is larger in diameter than salami is, and has a very distinctive pink colour, which comes from the saltpetre added during the curing process.

I eat mortadella served very thin, each slice almost as fine as a sheet of paper, whereas I cut my salami a few millimetres thick. In Bologna, salami is often served in cubes at the beginning of the meal and accompanied with a rustic bread.

Viva la Mortadella!

Restaurants | Famous Chefs:

La Villa Castagnola, Lugano

http://www.villacastagnola.com/

Carluccio's, UK

http://www.carluccios.com/

Morue

Brandade de morue is made from salted cod, milk (or thick cream, if you're feeling uninhibited), olive oil, lemon juice, garlic and herbs (thyme and laurel). Once the mixed puree becomes sufficiently unctuous, it is cooked as a gratin in the oven. The best brandades are airy and aromatic, smelling of their garlic and thyme and the salted cod.

Morue dates from the era before refrigerators, when the best method of conservation was salt, which Provence has in spades. (Unbleached grey salt from Guérande is perhaps the most famous: it is still harvested by hand, using pre-Roman methods.) Brandade de morue is first recorded in Nîmes, a landlocked city far enough from the sea that all saltwater fish had to be dried or salted. 'Morue' is French for salt cod; of course, fresh cod – *cabillaud* – is not found in the Mediterranean.

In the nineteenth century, Charles Durand, the archbishop of Alès' cook, concocted the *brandade* much as we know it today, by mixing salted cod with signature Provençal ingredients like olive oil, a little garlic, and thyme. Durand would stir the mixture with a wooden spoon; the Occitan verb is *brandar*, to stir vigorously – hence "brandade." Before the invention of the food processor, this dish was so labour intensive that it required two or three cooks to stir the thick mixture so that it could achieve its requisite fluffy lightness.

There are several variations on the traditional recipe: brandade with potato, which the original recipe lacked; and, for a more luxurious brandade, with truffles.

Brandade is a favourite among French politicians. One nineteenth century prime minister described it as "mankind's greatest achievement"; another claimed that when he ate *brandade* he could hear the crickets singing in the pines around the Magne tower.

In Provence, the brandade is as popular as tapenade and aioli: it is a kind of mousse spread on toast. Anticipating that first bite, is one of the most important moments in the day.

When I first arrived in Spain, I was surprised to see triangular salted cod hanging in fishmongers' windows. In Spain it is called *bacalao*, (*morue* in French), and the fish is gutted before being salted and dried on rocks or wooden racks. In Madrid I would often visit the famous fishmongers called La Casa del Bacalao, which I think was the best place to buy fresh salted cod.

Morue, salted cod, bacalao, *gadus morhua*: take your choice!

Recipes:

Brandade de morue recipe by Edouard Loubet

http://www.capelongue.com/uk

Restaurants | Famous Chefs:

La Casa del Bacalao, Madrid

http://madrid.salir.com/la_casa_del_bacalao-calle_del_carmen_20

Moscow Mule | Blood & Sand | Screwdriver by Eben Freeman

In Hong Kong I met Eben Freeman from New York's Tailor Restaurant and Bar. Eben is a pioneer of 'molecular mixology,' the application of science to cocktail making. Eben is the creator, among other edgy cocktails, of the Mojito of the Future, made with solidified pearls of mint and lime juice suspended in a jellied mixture of rum, sugar and soda.

When I told Eben about *The Curious Gourmand,* he shared some great stories of classic cocktails, stories that he has picked up during his career. Here are a few – but keep in mind that most are urban legends.

The Moscow Mule is made with vodka, ginger beer, sugar syrup and lime juice. It came about in the 1940s when John G. Martin of G. F. Heublein Brothers (a spirits and food distributor), and Jack Morgan, owner of the Cock'n Bull Tavern in Los Angeles, decided to create a cocktail to market Morgan's struggling Cock'n Bull ginger-beer franchise. The name refers to the vodka's Russian origin and the intense flavour kick of the ginger beer. This cocktail should be served in a copper cup.

The Blood and Sand is made with scotch, cherry brandy or beer, sweet vermouth and orange juice. The name comes from Vicente Blasco Ibáñez' novel *Sangre y arena*. The cocktail was supposedly created to celebrate the premiere of the 1922 film starring Rudolph Valentino, which was based on Ibáñez' book about a poor boy from Seville who becomes a famous toreador.

A Screwdriver is in itself a simple cocktail made with vodka and orange juice, which was first enjoyed in the 1950s, but its origin is rather unique. The story goes that some American engineers used to spike their canned orange juice with vodka and stir the concoction with their screwdrivers!

Eben and his friend Sam Mason, the ex-pastry chef of WD-50, (Willie Dufresne's New York restaurant known as a temple to molecular cuisine) were able to visit me while I lived in Hong Kong. They participated in a Childhood Memories Dinner that we held in the Mandarin Oriental's Krug Room. Freeman featured Brown Butter Rum, one of his signature cocktails; he invented it after tasting Mason's famous brown-butter ice cream. Eben borrowed Mason's technique called "fat washing," which consists of mixing melted fat with alcohol, chilling the mixture until the fat solidifies before skimming it off and infusing the whole into rum.

Thanks for the stories, Eben. See you back at the bar.

Recipe:

Blood and Sand recipe by Eben Freeman

http://www.epicurious.com/video/cocktails/cocktails-classics/1915458821/how-to-make-a-blood-and-sand-cocktail/10533570001

Note a Note

One of the highlights of my professional life to date was the visit of Hervé This to the Pierre Gagnaire restaurant in Hong Kong in the spring of 2009. Hervé This is a renowned French chemist who first brought science to the kitchen with molecular gastronomy. Molecular gastronomy is the scientific analysis of everyday culinary phenomena: from frying a steak (texture and colour change), to cooking an egg (liquid transformed to solid).

Pierre Gagnaire is a culinary wizard: he mixes flavours, tastes, textures and ingredients in startling ways. When I first ate at Gagnaire's Paris restaurant, I felt that I had just been born : never before had so many flavours burst in my mouth. Gagnaire famously dislikes the term 'molecular cuisine,' as he feels that it is prejudicial; he insists that his cooking isn't chemical, but just "follows This' techniques."

For This' Hong Kong visit, he and Gagnaire created the world's first menu made with entirely synthetic compounds. They called the menu *Note a Note*, in reference to the musician who composes 'note by note' to create a symphony. The menu's sections were named after famous chemists, like Jean-Antoine Nollet and Adolphe Wurtz. At the Mandarin, we were very cautious with how we discussed it in the press, though there were some jokes about it in Europe: "Is Gagnaire going to poison the Chinese?" The Cantonese are passionate about food, however, and every table was booked while the menu featured on Pierre's menu.

For Note a Note, This conceived a starter of jelly balls tasting of apple and lemon: "smooth, crusty, and frosty." This took ascorbic acid with apple juice in a glucose solution to make the apple pearls. Then, with the sugar substitute, glucose, he created a sugar galette; finally, he threw in some citric acid with some maltitol to create an effervescent lemon granité. No apples or lemons or caramels were used; only chemical imitations. Rather than using plant tissue, or meat, the chef "used reverse osmosis and fractionation to create compounds, building the dish in layers to include firmness, hardness, softness, stickiness, pungency and flavour."

This hoped the chemistry of Note A Note will open possibilities with applications outside the rarefied world of three-star restaurants. He says: "If we want to have a better environment, we have to help farmers behave more correctly, and in order to do that, they have to get richer by adding value. So instead of growing and selling carrots, they need to create compounds from them."

Every cook wants to change the world.

Recipes:

Note à Note recipe by Pierre Gagnaire

Restaurants | Famous Chefs:

Pierre, Pierre Gagnaire, Hong Kong

http://www.mandarinoriental.com/hongkong/dining/restaurants/pierre/

Opera / Éclair / Sarchertorte / Paris Brest Pastries

Who doesn't like desserts? As a child I often sneaked into the kitchen to eat cakes leftover from our family's Sunday lunch. While in primary school, I would use my pocket money to go to the pâtisserie across the church square near my school in Tassin la Demi-Lune. I would hover by the windows, devouring pastries with my eyes. Once I'd chosen, I would go in and buy a single pastry that I would eat while waiting for my parents to pick me up. I will tell you here the stories of my four favourites.

First, the Opera. It is made of six layers: three almond sponge (known as Joconde), coffee syrup, a bitter chocolate ganache; and a chocolate glaze as the final touch. The famous *pâtissier* Gaston Lenôtre has been credited with its invention, although the real creator was probably Cyriaque Gavillon, who worked for Dalloyau, the legendary Parisian gastronomic house. Gavillon wanted to create a dessert with visible layers, and one whose every ingredient could be tasted in each mouthful. His wife gave it the name "Opera," after a famous prima ballerina who used to come in the shop; she would practice her steps while waiting for her cake! The cake endured, even if the ballerina's name did not.

The éclair ('lightning bolt' in English) is another dessert I love : it is a slender choux pastry filled with cream and glazed with icing. The icing and cream have the same flavour – usually chocolate, vanilla or coffee.

Opera / Éclair / Sarchertorte / Paris Brest Pastries

Antonin Carême, the nineteenth century chef, is credited with the éclair's creation, perhaps at his pâtisserie de la rue de la Paix.

The Sachertorte is another classic chocolate cake that I'm fond of; it was invented by Franz Sacher (a sixteen years old trainee pastry chef) in 1832, to honour the famous Viennese politician Klemens Wenzel von Metternich. The recipe requires two layers of sponge cake with a thin layer of apricot jam in the middle and chocolate icing on top. The original recipe is kept in a safe in Vienna's famous Hotel Sacher.

The Paris-Brest is a ring shape pastry filled with praline cream and sprinkled with slivered almonds. It was created in 1910 by Louis Durand, a pastry chef in Maisons-Laffitte, north of Paris. The dessert was inspired by the famous cycling race between Paris and Brest, the regional capital of Brittany: the pastry's shape represents a bicycle wheel. The race runs 1,200 kilometres from Paris to Brest and back to Paris. Founded in 1891, it is the oldest bicycling event, and is held every four years. Luckily the Paris-Brest is available in pâtiseries all over France, all year round.

My thanks to Lenôtre, Gavillon, Sacher, Carême and Durand.

Recipes:

Opéra recipe by Gaston Lenôtre

http://www.nytimes.com/2009/01/09/dining/09lenotre.html?scp=53&sq=chocolate+recipes&st=nyt

Éclair recipe

http://www.foodtimeline.org/foodpies.html#eclairs

Sarchertorte recipe by Wolfgang Puck

http://www.foodnetwork.com/recipes/wolfgang-puck/wolfgangs-sachertorte-recipe/index.html

Paris Brest recipe

http://www.cuisine-french.com/cgi/mdc/l/en/recettes/paris_brest_ill.html

Restaurants | Famous Chefs:

Opéra

http://www.dalloyau.fr/

Sachertorte

http://www.sacher.com/

OREO

The Oreo must be one of the most recognized biscuits around the world; everyone knows its black and white colour and its blue cylindrical package.

The first Oreo was created in 1912 by New Jersey's National Biscuit Company (Nabisco).

For such a ubiquitous cookie, the name's origins are quite mysterious. Various etymologies have been given for the Oreo's name, though none are conclusive: Tom Diorio, a likely fictitious employee of Nabisco's, suggested the recipe, following one of his family's old recipes (a clear case of giving an upstart biscuit a fake pedigree, I think!). It's also possible that Oreo comes from "d'or," French for gold, because the Oreo's first packaging had the name printed in gold. A Nabisco spokesman suggested in the 1980s that the company's first chairman, Adolphus Green, was a classical scholar, and so named the cookie after the ancient Greek word for mountain (*oros*). That is perhaps the likeliest explanation, since the first cookies were shaped like mounds.

Ferran Adrià has created an Oreo starter – albeit one that's savoury (black olive biscuit bracketing crème fraiche) rather than sweet: once again the tongue confounds the eye.

At Hong Kong's Mandarin Grill + Bar, Oreo was our best selling dessert : made with oreo crumbles, topped with vanilla ice cream, and finally hot chocolate foam channelled through a siphon. The foam would melt the ice cream and turn the plate into a chocolate sea. A winner for the eyes and the mouth.

Oreo is the most popular biscuit around the world; its parent company Nabisco sells almost 7.5 billion cookies every year! In the France of my childhood, the most popular biscuit was the Prince (chocolate filled between two biscuit rings stamped with a Prince figure), Paille d'Or (raspberry filled Golden Stray) and Le Petit Écolier (The Little Schoolboy, a butter biscuit with chocolate on top). All three are produced by Lefèvre-Utile (LU), a manufacturer based in Nantes, now owned by Krafts Food.

What's your favourite biscuit?

Recipe:

Oreo recipe by Ferràn Adria

http://www.hungryinhogtown.com/hungry_in_hogtown/2007/06/i_believe_i_can.html

Restaurant | Famous Chef:

Oreo

http://www.nabiscoworld.com/oreo/

Ortolan

In 1995 the former president of France, François Mitterrand, ordered this endangered bird, small as a thumb, for his dinner on New Year's Eve. Terminally ill, Mitterrand chose never to eat again, and would die eight days later. Barbaric, cried some critics; his attempt to close his life with an immortal gesture, said his defenders.

The ortolan is a tiny songbird, which has been considered a delicacy for centuries among French gastronomes – it has been illegal to hunt, however, since 1998. I feel that my life in food will not be complete until I eat an ortolan. I would not break the law, of course, but if I am ever offered one, my curiosity will outweigh other considerations.

The lemon-coloured ortolan, known as a bunting in English, emigrates from Sweden to North Africa every year. It appears in French *chansons* as the symbol of innocence and of the love of Christ.

The traditional way to eat an ortolan is for the diner to cover his head with an embroidered cloth, so that none of the bird's flavours will be lost. (Some claim that the diner wishes to hide his gluttony from God; other, more sardonic wits cite how messy the meal is.) Only the bird's head should dangle out of the diner's lips; at last the head is bitten off, and usually discarded, though some do choose to eat it whole.

Captured alive, the ortolan is blinded and force fed for a month on millet, grapes and figs. This technique originated in the kitchens of classical Rome (see *Apicius*). After the ortolan has swollen to four times its original size, it is drowned alive in a snifter of Armagnac. The carcass is then cooked for eight minutes in an oven; when done it is immediately brought to the table.

The ortolan must rest on the tongue, while its roasted vapours are rapidly inhaled and fat cascades down the throat. When cool, it may take fifteen minutes to work through the breast and wings and into the organs, which burst with a flower-like liqueur.

Gourmets say that you can taste the bird's entire life.

Restaurant | Famous Chef:

Le Florida, Bernard Ramouneda, Castera-Verduzan

http://midipyrenees.angloinfo.com/afdetail.asp?Rec=2887

Oscar Tschirsky
Waldorf Salad | Egg Benedict | Thousand Island Dressing

L et's review the ingredients of this well-known dish. The original Waldorf Salad included celery, grapes, apple and mayonnaise, all served on a bed of lettuce. Walnuts, now standard, were actually a later addition.

This salad was created in the 1890s by the Maître d´Hôtel of the Waldorf Hotel, Oscar Tschirsky, and quickly became a classic, celebrated in the Cole Porter song, *You're the Top* (and mentioned rather more snidely in an episode of *Fawlty Towers*). Modern versions sometimes substitute different fruit or dressing; they may also include chicken or turkey to make a more substantial meal.

Another dish Tschirsky is said to have created is Eggs Benedict, in a story recounted in the December 1942 edition of *The New Yorker*. The "Talk of the Town" column gives this version: a Wall Street banker – Lemuel Benedict – wandered into the Waldorf one morning in 1894 with an appalling hangover. He ordered buttered toast, poached eggs, crisp bacon, topped off with "a hooker of hollandaise sauce" to settle his stomach and quiet his aching head. Tschirsky liked his Eggs Benedict so much that he added the dish to the Waldorf's breakfast and luncheon menu; but he first substituted English muffins (newly introduced from England, and considered a delicacy) for the toast, and ham for the bacon.

Like the Waldorf Salad, Eggs Benedict quickly gained a following, and is now one of the most famous of brunch dishes.

Oscar Tschirsky is credited with the invention of several other dishes. Most memorably, he refined what we now know as Thousand Island Dressing. Tradition mentions that Sophia Lalonde, wife of a fishing guide on New York state's Thousand Islands archipelago, passed the recipe to a prominent actress, May Irwin. By strange coincidence, Irwin was also a cookbook writer; she gave the secret of Thousand Island to George Boldt, who happened to own the Waldorf Astoria Hotel. Boldt then asked Tschirsky to add it to the menu. The dressing consists of mayonnaise, ketchup, tabasco and chopped pickles, onions, red peppers, green olives and hard-boiled eggs. It was a keeper.

In 1896, Tschirsky published a 900-page cookery collection of famous chefs' recipes : *The Cookbook, by 'Oscar' of the Waldorf*. Tschirsky himself reportedly couldn't cook anything more complicated than scrambled eggs.

Thank you, Mr. Tschirsky!

Recipe:

Eggs Benedict

Restaurant | Famous Chef:

The Cook Book, by 'Oscar' of the Waldorf

Oysters & Pearls

While working at Terence Conran's Bluebird Restaurant in London, I once saw a customer find a pearl inside an oyster that he was eating: an extremely rare event. I hope that she kept it and had a necklace made out of it.

Every oyster produces a substance called mother-of- pearl, or nacre, which is a combination of calcium carbonate and the mineral aragonite. This substance protects the oyster's soft body from impurities that may slip in when an oyster opens itself to breathe or eat. The oyster isolates such impurities by producing nacre around it. A pearl necklace with gems of graduated size is called a "fall," whereas one with pearls of uniform size is a "choker."

For November 2010, I invited Thomas Keller, one of only three living chefs who hold a double Michelin 3-star rating, to Hong Kong's Mandarin Oriental. He prepared one of his signature dishes, "Oysters and Pearls": Malpeque oyster, small pearl tapioca, milk, heavy cream, crème fraiche, ground black pepper, salt and large egg yolks for the sabayon. The sauce is made with dry vermouth, minced shallots, white wine vinegar, unsalted butter and minced chives. The whole is topped up with some oscietra caviar.

Ferran Adrià has even created an edible 'pearl': oyster juice solidified until it forms a large shimmering sphere! This culinary process was pioneered in the 1990s and is now known as 'spherification,' which consists of transforming any liquid into a round shape. The liquid may be fruit, vegetable or even oyster juice, which is mixed with sodium alginate, a type of algae-based gelling agent. The mixture is then piped into a syringe (thus sucking up the tiniest droplets) into a bath of calcium chloride solution. The drops jellify on contact with the liquid, and become crispy on the outside while their centres remain liquid.

Moleculary yours…

Recipe:

Oysters & Pearls recipe by Thomas Keller

http://www.epicurious.com/recipes/food/views/Oysters-and-Pearls-105859

Restaurant | Famous Chef:

The French Laundry, Thomas Keller, Yountville

http://www.frenchlaundry.com/

Pacojet

Ask any contemporary chef what essential equipment a kitchen should have, and I can predict the answer; the ascetic purist will insist that anything is possible with good knives and pots. The more provocative will joke, "A cryovac, of course! And a volcano vaporizer!" But most chefs working today agree that the pacojet, invented in the late 1980s, is necessary in the professional kitchen.

The machine – essentially a food processor – was created in Switzerland, its original intent "to pulverize mice into laboratory sausage for medical students." It looks rather like an old coffee machine: shaped like a tower, it includes a plastic jug which holds a chrome steel container. It also has blades that can cut frozen food at 2000 RPMs, in shavings as fine as 2 microns thick.

The pacojet has revolutionized the creation of purées, soups, and sorbets; it is especially good for finely slicing substances that freeze too hard – both savoury and low glycaemic mixtures. It works by making ice cream in reverse, through a process of reconstitution by taking frozen ice cream and churning (pacotizing) it to a fresh, creamy texture.

A cook slices the main ingredients; places them in a chrome steel beaker; adds liquid; and then freezes the whole. For sorbets, soups or purées, place the beaker under the blade, and key in the number of portions desired. The pacojet's design reduces waste, since a cook can use up portions of a frozen mixture without thawing all of it.

Its patent was bought in the late 1980s by Gunter Scheible, who was a marketing expert and consultant at the time. He had been asked to review the development of a mounted Black and Decker drill that had a blade attachment. Its patent was held by Switzerland's Patent Corporation (Paco); one of Scheible's associates suggested the 'jet' suffix, because of the machine's speed. The name was scribbled on a cocktail napkin and has stuck ever since.

For my own dream kitchen, I would like to own a Pacojet along with a

Thermomix, the only food processor that can weigh, blend, grind, knead, steam and cook…

Recipe:

Green Asparagus Sorbet

Restaurant | Famous Chef:

http://pacojet.mesotronic.ch

Paella

I love eating paella on Sundays; it's a great dish to eat *en famille*. During my six years in Spain I ate many delicious paellas, though my favourites were from Valencia, where the first paella is recorded.

Paella is made with short grain white rice, chicken, beans, paprika, saffron, garlic, salt, olive oil, string beans and water. You will never find seafood in a true Valencian paella, though on occasion it may include game (hare or wild duck). I've also eaten it with snails.

The name comes from the Catalan word for the large flat pan (*patella*, from the Latin*)*, in which paella is cooked. So, in Valencia any pan is a paella, though in Latin America a pan is called *paellera*. Though its name comes from Latin, paella also reflects Spain's Arabic history, when cooks would bulk out leftovers (*baqiyah*) with rice, which the Arabs introduced to Europe.

A paella stands or falls by the texture of its rice, which must be the short-grained variety; for true authenticity, try to find a Valencian *granza*. "In Spain, paella is not fluffy (like a pilaf) or oozy (like a risotto.) Instead, it is somewhere in between, slightly creamy, glistening…" The main flavours will come from the *sofrito* (onions cooked until golden, with garlic and peppers). And remember not to stir paella; instead give the pan a shake lest you break the sheen that coats the rice grains.

It is documented that before the eighteenth century, Valencian paella was made with rice-filled rodent meat (*rata de marjal*), a 'delicacy' still eaten in the Philippines, Thailand and Cambodia. In Valencia, rabbit later replaced the meat.

To follow the traditional Valencian method, heat virgin olive oil in a pan, sauté the seasoned meat, and add vegetables. Then add garlic, tomatoes and beans; then paprika, saffron and water. Boil the mixture until it has been reduced by half; finally, add rice and simmer until it has finished cooking.

Gourmets consider the sticky rice near the top of the pan to be a delicacy.

Que aprovechen!

Recipe:

Chicken & Prawn Paella

Restaurant | Famous Chef:

Casa Moro, 250-1

Pastis

I could say that pastis is my preferred aperitif, but it is only at its best when drunk in Provence during mid-summer. I like to sip it in the shadow of an olive tree while the crickets are singing.

The word pastis comes from the Occitan *passe-sitis* (*passe-soif*) meaning "to slake the thirst." Pastis is a liqueur made with anise and is served as an aperitif diluted one part to five parts of water. It is true that pastis (also called *pastaga*) does not taste the same if drunk anywhere else.

Pastis became popular following the ban on absinthe in 1915. The main producer of absinthe, Jules Pernod, then started producing his liqueur without wormwood; he kept, however, the star anise, herbs and liquorice.

But it was Pernod's main competitor, Ricard, who first used the word "pastis." Some people say that it might come from the Italian word *pistacchio*, meaning "mix," due to the water combined with the liqueur.

The two rival companies merged into Pernod Ricard in 1975 and have now become the second largest alcoholic beverage company in the world. Pernod-Ricard owns such famous brands as Absolut, Chivas, Havana Club, Champagne Mumm, and Perrier-Jouët. My best friend Nicolas Payet runs the Portugal branch, and we always share a 102 when we see each other: we have a double portion of Ricard 51 (representing 1951, the year it was created).

There is a legend I love about the origin of pastis. A hermit in Provence's Luberon mountains was known for living in his wooden hut surrounded by plants and herbs. When plague struck the region, the hermit was miraculously unaffected. He then shared his beverage with those who had been struck down; they recovered.

There are many variations of pastis, such as the Mauresque (in reference to the Moors), which is served with orgeat syrup; the Tomate, with grenadine syrup; and the Perroquet (Parrot), with green mint syrup.

Proust had his madeleine, which brought back so many memories of his childhood; I have my Pastis, and the sound of the crickets. In Provence, the crickets start to sing at 26C ° degrees; they are like an alarm clock to remind us that it is the perfect temperature to have a Pastis!

Based on the *Farmers' Almanac*, you can use a cricket to tell the temperature in degrees C by counting the number of chirps in 25 seconds, dividing this number by 3 and then adding 4.

Restaurant | Famous Chef:

Pernod Ricard group

http://www.pernod-ricard.com/

Pastis restaurant, Ibiza

http://pastisibiza.com/

Peach Melba & Pear Belle Hélène

The following two desserts have disappeared from menus in recent times. But their names alone remind me of traditional Sunday lunches in formal restaurants with my grandfather Georges Melon, the family patriarch. He would sit at the head of the table with his children crowding around, and the grandchildren at the other end of the table.

I am not sure why modern tastes have banished both Peach Melba and Pear Belle Hélène from dessert menus. Perhaps they are due to be rediscovered and reinterpreted. Both desserts have the same creator, August Escoffier. Escoffier, whose mentor was Antoine Carême, is the father of the modern kitchen. He was first to organize his staff by 'brigades,' with each section run by its own *chef de partie*, and to serve meals in courses. Escoffier is also famous for his reference book *Le Guide Culinaire*, and for opening various Ritz Hotels with business partner Cesar Ritz.

It was during the first collaboration in London's Savoy Hotel that Escoffier invented the Peach Melba. This dessert consists of a poached peach topped with raspberry sauce drizzled over vanilla ice cream. Escoffier created the dish to honour the Australian opera singer, Nellie Melba, who was performing in Wagner's opera *Lohengrin*, which features an enchanted swan. On the night the Peach Melba made its debut, Escoffier presented it in a swan-shaped ice sculpture; he called it *pêche au cygne*. The first recipe did not include raspberries; Escoffier later added that fruit, whose tartness balances the peach's sweetness, and renamed it "Peach Melba."

Escoffier was so found of Nellie Melba that he also created a toast named after her. Melba toast accompanies soups or salads and consists of toasted bread with the crusts cut off, and then cut into triangles. The triangles are then toasted a final time under the grill until they turn golden and their edges curl.

Pear Belle Hélène, another Escoffier dessert, is made with poached pear on vanilla ice cream topped with chocolate syrup. Again, this sweet had a musical inspiration: Escoffier created it after seeing a production of Offenbach's *La Belle Hélène*. The original recipe included crystallized violets, now a somewhat rarefied ingredient, though it was popular among nineteenth century confectioners. Thomas Keller of the French Laundry has created a sophisticated modern Pear Belle Hélène, with chocolate fondant pudding, pear sorbet, and a caramelized slice of pear.

Bravo, Mlles Melba et Hélène!

Recipe:

Belle Hélène Pear

Restaurant | Famous Chef:

Thomas Keller, *The French Laundry Cookbook*

Personalities

Before beginning work on *The Curious Gourmand*, I always wondered why so many soups, creams, sauces, potatoes carried the name of a famous personality: perhaps a writer, a member of one of Europe's royal families, or an army general.

Some of these personalities were gourmets and regulars in famous restaurants; others were chefs, culinary artists in their own right, who gave their creations their own names. In the future, we might have a sauce Macron or *soppa di Berlusconi*.

Agnes Sorel

* (1422-1450); mistress of King Charles VII of France.

* A poultry based velouté with a mushroom stock garnished with shredded poultry meat, pickled beef tongue and mushrooms. Its less grandiose name is 'cream of chicken soup'!

Alexandra

* (1844-1925) British queen consort and wife of King Edward VII.

* Dessert made with mixed fruits in kirsch nestled on strawberry ice.

* Consommé thickened with tapioca flour, garnished with shredded poultry meat and a lettuce chiffonade.

Balzac

* Honoré de Balzac (1799-1850), French novelist. The writer was

a regular at the Very restaurant, which specialized in soups. One of the first restaurants in Paris, the Very was near the Palais Royal, and later merged with its neighbour the Grand Véfour.

* A barley cream soup garnished with shredded celery and leeks.

Béchamel

* Louis de Béchamel (1630-1703), marquis de Nointel, financier and patron of the arts.

* A white sauce, one of the base sauces of French cuisine, consisting of white roux (butter and flour) with milk stirred into it. The marquis himself is said to have created this sauce; the béchamel evolved from a velouté of veal with lashings of cream added.

Brillat-Savarin

* Jean Anthelme Brillat-Savarin (1755-1826); French lawyer and politician, as well gastronomic expert; author of *The Physiology of Taste*.

* A soft white crust cow's milk cheese.

* A cake called Savarin, a type of baba without raisins.

BYRON

* George Gordon Byron, (1788-1824); English poet.

* Potatoes covered with cheese and cooked as a gratin.

Choisy

* François-Timoléon Choisy (1644-1724), priest and prolific author; hero of many infamous amorous adventures.

* Garnish for fish poached in white wine sauce and shredded lettuce and truffles.

Chateaubriand

* François-René de Chateaubriand (1768-1848), French vicomte, writer, politician and diplomat.

* A thick cut of beef tenderloin. It is usually served grilled and accompanied by a sauce, either béarnaise, Choron, or bordelaise. The dish was dreamed up by Chateaubriand's personal chef Montmireil.

Choron

* Alexandre Étienne Choron (1837-1924), French chef at the restaurant Voisin, which was on the rue Saint Honoré. Choron is remembered for serving animals from the local zoo – elephant, wolf, and bear – during the 1870 siege of Paris when the Prussians had encircled the city.

* Béarnaise sauce accompanied by tomato.

Colbert

* Jean-Baptiste Colbert (1619-83); Louis XIV's finance minister.

* Consommé made with sliced poached eggs.

* Fried eggs with grilled sausages.

* Battered fish fried and served with maître d'hôtel butter (whipped butter mixed with chopped parsley, lemon juice, salt, pepper, and Worcestershire sauce).

* Maître d'hôtel butter with meat glaze and chopped tarragon.

* Tournedos accompanied with poultry croquettes, fried eggs and truffle slices.

Cumberland

* Prince William, Duke of Cumberland (1721-1765), the third son of King George II of England.

* Famous sausage.

* Sauce made with red currant jelly in port wine, mustard with shredded orange and lemon peel.

* Sauce that accompanies venison, ham or lamb; it was created in Hanover, where the duke was stationed during the Seven Years' War.

Demidov

* Count Anatole Demidov (1813-70), industrialist, diplomat and arts patron. Russian by nationality, he was resident in Paris.
* Chicken Demidov is stuffed and fried with turnips, carrots and truffles.

Derby

* Edward Smith-Stanley (1752-1834), Lord Derby, English statesman who founded the Epsom Oaks horse races.
* Chicken Derby, *foie gras* and truffles with a creamed demi-glaze sauce, in a casserole stuffed with rice.
* A rice and onion cream soup with curry.

Doria

* Ancient Genovese noble family.
* *Printanier* consommé with cucumbers and quenelles.
* Cucumber velouté. Invented by the Swiss chef Sally Weil (1896-1976) at a hotel in Yokohama, Japan.

Dubarry

* Jeanne Bécu (1743-93); comtesse du Barry, mistress of King Louis XV. She used cauliflower to whiten her powdered wigs.
* A cauliflower cream soup.

Dugléré

* Adolphe Dugléré, student of Antonin Carême and head chef at the Café Anglais in Paris.
* Poached fish in a white wine sauce with crushed tomatoes.

Grimaldi

* An aristocratic Genoese family, whose descendants include Monaco's King Albert II.

* A consommé made with tomato stock garnished with shredded celery.

* Bombe Grimaldi, frozen kummel flavoured dessert.

Lucullus

* Lucius Licinius Lucullus (157-118 BCE) Roman general renowned for his household's excellent cuisine. He is credited with introducing the cherry and apricot to Rome.

* Tournedos with sliced truffle, mushrooms, asparagus tips and a *perigueux* sauce.

Margot

* Marguerite de Valois (1553-1615); first wife of Henry IV of France.

* Reine Margot soup, made with poultry and almond milk.

Margherita of Savoy

* Margherita Maria Teresa Giovanna of Savoy (1851-1926); Queen Consort of Umberto I.

* Neapolitan pizza topped with tomatoes, mozzarella and basil.

Marie-Louise

* Marie Louise of Austria (1791-1847), second wife of Napoleon I.

* A poultry velouté with barley cream garnished with *brunoise* diced vegetables.

Marigny

* Abel-François Poisson de Vandières (1727-81), vicomte de Marigny; brother of the marquise de Pompadour, who was mistress to Louis XV.

* Velouté made from a purée of green peas garnished with French beans and sorrel sprigs.

Mary Stewart

* (1542-87); queen of France and later queen of Scotland.
* A poultry cream garnished with carrots and fresh green peas.

Massena

* André Masséna (1758-1817), prince of Essling and Marshal of France.
* Poached eggs with artichoke hearts, slices of bone marrow and a tomato flavoured béarnaise sauce.
* Tournedos with artichoke hearts filled with asparagus tips.

Matignon

* Charles Auguste de Goÿon de Matignon (1607-75); marshal of France under Louis XIV.
* Tournedos with a vegetable *paysanne*, mushrooms, truffles and thin *frites*.

Melon

* Antoine Marc Bodhant (1972-); restaurateur and author of *The Curious Gourmand*.
* White grape grown in Burgundy and the Loire Valley, also known as Muscadet.

Mirabeau

* Honoré Gabriel Riqueti (1749-91); French count, writer and orator.
* Tournedos Mirabeau, which consists of anchovy fillets, olives, tarragon and thin *frites*.

Mirepoix

* Charles-Pierre-Gaston-Francois de Lévis (1699-1757); duke of Lévis-Mirepoix, marshal of France under Louis XV.

* Base for stocks and soups: two parts onion, one part carrot and one part celery.

Mornay

* Philippe de Mornay (1549-1623), friend of France's Henry IV, nicknamed 'the Huguenots' Pope.' Nineteenth century chef Joseph Voiron invented a sauce and named it after the son of one of his cooks, Mornay.

* White roux with milk stirred (béchamel) with grated cheese (either Gruyère or Emmenthal) added.

Nelson

* Horatio Nelson, Viscount Nelson (1758-1805); British admiral who defeated the French at the battle of Trafalgar.

* Soup made from fish stock garnished with rice and cubes of lobster or poached fish with white wine sauce, glazed and garnished with *noisette* potatoes.

Pavlova

*Pavlova, Anna (1881-1931); Russian ballerina.

* Dessert made of meringue, topped up with Chantilly cream, and fruits, usually strawberries, bananas, kiwis, or peaches.

Pozharsky

* Dmitry Mikhailovich Pozharsky (1578-1642); Russian prince whose sobriquet was 'Saviour of the Motherland.'

* Veal finely minced, mixed with breadcrumbs and cream, formed into cutlets and fried.

POMPADOUR

* Jeanne-Antoinette Poisson (1721-64) mistress of France's Louis XV, who gave her the title Marquise de Pompadour.

* Velouté of tomatoes garnished with shredded lettuce and sago.

RABELAIS

* François Rabelais (1494-1553); priest, doctor, great writer and gastronome.

* Consommé garnished with carrots, turnips and truffles.

* Lampray eel à la Rabelais, created by Charles Ranhofer, nineteenth century chef at New York's Delmonico restaurant, and author of *The Epicurean*.

RICHELIEU

* Armand-Jean du Plessis (1585-1642) cardinal-duc de Richelieu; prime minister under Louis XIII.

* Consommé with chicken dumpling and garnished with shredded carrot and lettuce.

ROMANOV

* Imperial Russian family (1613-1917).

* Vanilla ice cream with strawberries flavoured with liqueur and Chantilly cream.

ROTHSCHILD

* European banking dynasty.

* Soufflé made with orange liquor, pineapple and strawberries. Antonin Carême created this dessert for Baron James Mayer de Rothschild.

SANDWICH

* John Montagu, (1718-92) Earl of Sandwich and Lord of the

Admiralty;

* Two slices of bread enclosing a savoury filling.

SÉVIGNÉ

* Marie de Rabutin-Chantal (1626-96); marquise de Sévigné, famous for her letters to her daughter, a correspondence which lasted 25 years. It was she who recounted the death of François Vatel.

* Consommé with asparagus tips, shredded lettuce and poultry quenelles.

SOUBISE

* Charles de Rohan (1715-1787), prince de Soubise; Marshal of France and friend of Louis XV.

* French white onion sauce created by Soubise's chef Constant.

SUVOROV

* Alexander Vasilyevich Suvorov (1729-1800); Russian general.

* Pheasant or woodcock stuffed with *foie gras* and truffles, and cooked in a casserole which is sealed with pastry around the edge of the lid.

VALOIS

* French royal family (1328-1589).

* Béarnaise with meat glaze.

* Tournedos with chopped artichoke hearts and *pommes Anna* (thinly sliced potatoes, set in a mould, baked as a cake).

Pistou / Pesto

Pistou sauce comes from my adopted home, Provence, whereas pesto comes from Liguria on Italy's northwest coast. The two are often confused, with good reason, since though their names differ, both contain the same ingredients! The closeness of Provençal and Genoese cuisines is perhaps not surprising, given their proximity of Provence and northern Italy, and the cultural and trading links that have existed since pre-Roman times. The town of Nice itself has been part of France only since 1860. It previously belonged to the Italian statelet of Piedmont.

Pesto comes from the past participle *pesta* ("to crush"), in reference to its ground basil, pine nuts, grated *Parmigiano Reggiano* (or pecorino) and olive oil. The sauce originated in Genoa, where basil was introduced from North Africa. The Genoese serve pesto with minestrone in terracotta bowls called *xatte*.

West of Genoa, along the Ligurian coast, basil also proliferates throughout Provence, home of *pistou*. *Pistou* likely was adapted from pesto, though it perhaps tilts more toward garlic than its Italian cousin. As with pesto, *pistou* is used to give complexity and flavour to soups – tomato, leek, or potato. Pistou is also used in a delicious vegetable soup (known rather unimaginatively as *la soupe au pistou*), which is very similar to minestrone. Pistou is also served with roast lamb, pasta, and as a dip for crudités. Remember that the best way to store pistou is in an air-tight refrigerated container; drizzle the pistou with olive oil to prevent oxidation.

Nowadays there are many variations on pesto. Basil is often replaced with other herbs – arugula, perhaps, or mint – and the pine nuts with walnuts or cashews (both are cheaper than the *pignons.*) You can also find red pesto that was made from either sundried tomatoes or red bell peppers.

You say pesto, I say pistou…

Recipe:

Soupe au pistou, *The Complete Robuchon*, 678

Restaurant | Famous Chef:

Hotel Mas dou Pastre, Eygalières

http://masdupastre.com/lieu.htm

Pizza

Everybody loves a pizza. My favourite is the margherita. I find the simplicity of its three ingredients irresistible: basil, which is excellent for digestion; a little acidic tomato, high in vitamin C; and the creamy, smooth mozzarella.

The Margherita was invented in 1889 by Raffaele Esposito to honour Marguerite of Savoy (see *Personalities*). The queen's namesake pizza has the same three colours (green, white, red) as the Italian flag. Such nationalism was appropriate, since, as one expert claims, pizza has been "part of the Italian diet since the Stone Age."

The word *pizza* is a corruption of the Latin word *placenta*. A Roman dish, placenta was "a pie made of the finest flours, a topping of cheese mixed with honey, and a seasoning of bay leaves and oil." Baked on a hearth floor beside burning wood, placenta became charred (in Latin, *picea*) from the burning ashes; pizza is a dialect corruption of *picea*.

Italian pizza reflects the influence of two different cultures: the Etruscan and the Greek. The Etruscan prototype pizza was "a crude bread baked beneath the stones of a fire." Once the bread was cooked, the Etruscans added toppings; this version evolved into what we know as *focaccia*. In *The Aeneid*, Vergil describes the Trojans – emigrants from Asia Minor – using their loaves as edible plates, or trenchers.

Centuries later, when the Greeks colonized what is now Calabria, Apulia and Sicily, they introduced the concept of adding toppings on the bread *before* it was cooked. From these two influences, Italy now has "hundreds of styles and variations of pizza, which vary from region to region and even from town to town."

Naples is considered as the birthplace of the modern pizza. The city has many beautiful woodfired ovens made of Vesuvian rock. Tomatoes flourish in the Neapolitan climate and rich soil, and buffalo provide unparalleled mozzarella and *burrata*. Finally, the region's durum wheat flour provides the perfect base. It required only the *pizzaiolo*, the pizza artist, to bring these ingredients together and make magic with them…

As a good friend of mine says, colours often matter as much as taste, particularly when the red, green and white pay respect to *Il Tricolore!*

Recipe:	**Restaurant	Famous Chef:**
Margarita recipe	*Dean & Deluca*, 106-7

Pomme Purée

For me there are only two recipes in the world for *purée de pomme de terre*: my grandmother's and Joël Robuchon's. Mashed potatoes, as Americans know them, may be a culinary cliché, but there is an elegance to their simplicity. I will always remember the version served at Robuchon's L'Atelier in Paris.

As a child, I would help Mamie make her *purée*. We would boil unpeeled potatoes (Mamie favours the Bintje floury ones), and then plunge them into cold water. I would then peel the still hot potatoes and pass them through a masher. Mamie added some butter and hot milk while whipping the mass to incorporate air in order to make her *pommes* lighter.

To date only Joël Robuchon's recipe competes with Mamie's version for my affections. Mamie used a *tamis*, or drum sieve, to give her mashed potatoes a velvety consistency. Robuchon recommends using Ratte potatoes for their high starch content. Compared with the Russet, Ratte potatoes have a unique nutty flavour and whip up into a buttery texture. Robuchon also advises that cooks salt the cooking water when it is still cold; also, use a potato ricer instead of a food processor. The *purée de pommes de terre* from Robuchon is so exquisite that it rises above its state as a mere garnish or side order; it steals the scene and becomes the main dish!

Mashed potatoes are normally the perfect accompaniment to wintry meat dishes like beef daube. It also goes well with game, such as stews of venison or boar or hare civet. My brother-in-law Nicolas Sibille is what I would call a genuine hunter: he himself cooks all the game he brings home. For family Christmas dinners, Nicolas prepares delicious terrines accompanied by Mamie's famous *pommes.*

There are innumerable variations on *purée de pommes de terre,* but the one that I would like to recommend is crushed potato with butter cubes and Guérande rock salt sprinkled on top. You can use the tines of your fork to mash butter and salt together to get the buttery texture you want.

Pomme purée is another of my 'madeleines.' Whenever I hear the word, my grandmother rises before my eyes. I see her preparing the *purée,* shaping it into a little volcano on my plate, then tipping the meat juices inside until the lava flowed down my plate.

Mamie's kitchen will always be my Combray.

Recipe:

The Complete Robuchon, 623

Restaurant | Famous Chef:

Joël Robuchon

http://www.joel-robuchon.net/

Pomodoro

The tomato is probably my favourite vegetable, not just because you can prepare it in so many different ways, but also because when it first arrived in Europe, it was known as the 'love apple,' since the tomato's looks were so unearthly, and its flavours so intense, that it could only have come from Eden.

We should not, however, call a tomato a vegetable, because of course it is an edible fruit! Tomatoes are classed as berries of the flowering plant *solanum lycopersicum* (its botanical name means 'wolf peach').

The Spanish colonials borrowed the word tomato from the Aztec (Nahuatl) word *tomatl*. According to *The Cambridge World History of Food,* there was actually understandable confusion about what a tomato really was, since its appearance varies so widely. The Aztec capital's great Tlatelolco market sold tomatoes in diverse profusion: large, small, green, thin, sweet, large serpent tomatoes, nipple-shaped tomatoes, coyote tomatoes, and sand tomatoes…

While sixteenth century Flemish botanist Rembert Dodoens named the tomato the *poma amoris* (love apple), to the Italians it has always been the *pomi d'oro*, or golden apple, one of those fruits believed to grow in the fabled Hesperides, which were the classical Greek equivalent of paradise. In Italy, the tomato was first treated as an ornamental plant, because early on it was misclassified as a relative of the poisonous mandrake family. Also, the tomato neither looked like nor tasted like any other vegetable known and used by the Italians, since "it had a strange texture and consistency.

They were too acid to be eaten while green and looked spoiled when they were soft and ripe." But when the Italians finally incorporated the tomato into their cuisine, it was the beginning of an epic love affair; I think they should have kept Dodoens' term, *poma amoris,* after all!

The potato fared rather better (see *Frites*), despite its bad looks: dull, brown, heavy-on-the belly, it quickly sated whoever ate it. The Inca name, *papa*, is also the word for pope in Italian, and – literally translated – the "pope-ato" became the pope's fruit.

So, when you next bite a tomato, be careful that you don't lose your innocence and get thrown out of the Garden!

Recipe:

Tomato sauce recipe by Antonio Carluccio

http://www.antonio-carluccio.com/172

Popcorn

Popcorn evokes strong passions, despite being such an airy food. In her classic book *The Story of Corn,* Betty Fussell sums up the emotional response to it: "Popcorn connects toddlers and grannies, hard-hats and connoisseurs, moviegoers and sports fans, beer drinkers and teetotallers… cops and robbers, cowboys and Indians. Popcorn bags the past with the present and evokes even in old age the memories of childhood. We eat it not because it's good for us… but because it's joke food, and Americans love joke food. We eat popcorn for fun."

Popcorn's history is ancient: it dates back more than 5,000 years to prehistoric Mexico. The best current archaeological evidence comes from cobs excavated in Coxcatlin Cave in the Tehuacán Valley (southeast of Mexico City). The ears on this prehistoric corn were quite diminutive; each was slender as a pencil, with tiny little kernels lined up in rows of four and eight. Today's conventional corn may have more than a thousand kernels on the cob.

Both Christopher Columbus and Hernan Cortez write about popcorn in their diaries, recording how indigenous people used it as jewellery. One sixteenth-century Spanish priest described Aztec women wearing popcorn garlands in the hair "like orange blossoms, which they called *mumuchitl.*"

The two main popcorn varietals are the pointy grained "rice" and the more rounded "pearl." Each kernel contains both moisture and oil. When heated, the moisture becomes pressurized steam, trapped within the "starch-protein matrix until it suddenly explodes."

With its interesting texture, amorphous shape and capacity to serve as a blank canvas for stronger flavours, from caramel to chili, popcorn is a perfect ingredient for molecular gastronomy. It was perhaps inevitable that it should evolve from the Depression-era subsistence food to end up on the tables of four-star restaurants. Alinea's Grant Achatz serves liquefied caramel popcorn in tall shot glasses; Moto's Homaru Cantu serves a chilled corn soup paired with Mexican truffle under a sprinkling of frozen popcorn. And at his Los Angeles restaurant The Bazaar, José Andres, one of Ferran Adrià's acolytes, reinvented it as "Dragon's Breath": skewers of caramel popcorn plunged into a bowl filled with liquid nitrogen. A diner eats a skewer, and then breathes in through the nose; smoke then pours out the nostrils. Dragon's Breath became perhaps too successful – Andres withdrew it, "except for rare occasions… All of a sudden, it becomes like McDonald's. Everyone expects it! It's not good and fun anymore."

But however intellectual the approach to these dishes are, popcorn's enduring appeal is homely. As one of The Bazaar's diners said wistfully, "My favourite dishes are the ones that trigger a childhood memory. The caramel popcorn bites cooked in liquid nitrogen, the chicken croquette that looks like a Tater Tot (but tastes like a chicken pot pie), the cotton candy foie gras that's rolled in crushed corn nuts. I hadn't had traditional caramel popcorn or cotton candy since I was a kid, and if it wasn't for this molecular cooking, I wouldn't have cared."

Recipe:

Caramel popcorn by Grant Achatz

http://www.washingtonpost.com/wp-dyn/content/story/2008/12/02/ST2008120202754.html

Restaurant | Famous Chef:

Alinea, Grant Achatz, Chicago

http://www.alinearestaurant.com/

Pretzel

No bar can do without pretzels, because their saltiness makes customers thirsty. All those complimentary snacks are laid on to make you stay longer and drink more! But who would have thought that a bar snack had religious origins?

The pretzel dates from the Middle Ages, when a priest in a northern Italian monastery would bake bread from leftover dough. He then offered it as a treat for children who had memorized Bible verses and prayers. In Italian *pretiola* means "little reward." The three-loop knot thus supposedly represents the childrens' arms, folded in prayer – hence the modern Italian word for pretzel, *brachiola*. The three holes also represent the Trinity: The Father, Son and the Holy Ghost.

From northern Italy, the pretzel spread throughout Austria and Germany, where it was usually a sweet rather than a savoury snack; it also acquired the name *brezeln,* which became 'pretzel' in English.

The pretzel entered into religious tradition: it may be eaten for dinner on Good Friday as an alternative to eggs and dairy products, traditionally forbidden during Lent. Pretzels were formerly even hidden during Easter, just like eggs!

Why, you may wonder, are pretzels dark brown on the outside, but white in the middle? The colour comes from the egg yolk brushed over the dough before the pretzel is baked; the direct heat cooks the egg yolk until it becomes dark.

As for bar snacks, I myself have stopped eating peanuts after reading a report claiming that on average seven strains of urine can be found on them. Enough said! I prefer the Spanish tradition of offering tapas (*see Tapas*) for each drink you order : that tradition is a brilliant way to showcase the kitchen's creativity. It is far more interesting than the standard offerings of synthetic crisps or wasabi nuts.

Recipe:

Pretzel recipe

http://www.thefreshloaf.com/recipes/pretzels

Raised Finger

As a child, my ideas about foreign countries were greatly influenced by clichés from television programs, and misinformation passed between teenagers. For French students of my generation, England was the country where "my tailor is rich," because that was the first English sentence we learned. English policemen were called Bobbies. Oh, and people of good breeding always ate with their little fingers crooked.

Have you ever laughed at an upper-class Englishman drinking tea with his little finger raised? You might have thought that he was being pretentious. But the rationale behind his mannerism dates from the Middle Ages, when lords would eat with their fingers since the fork was not yet widely available (see *Fork*). Therefore, to season their food with salt and pepper, the nobility would always keep one or two fingers grease-free; they could then pick up salt and sugar more easily. A cultured person would eat with three fingers; a commoner would eat with five.

This is how the custom of raising the little finger came to distinguish classes in England.

Other protocols of English tea etiquette include placing the teaspoon on top of the teacup, or across the saucer, to signal the hostess that she should not pour you more tea. When seated at table, you may raise only your teacup, but when seated on a lounge, you should hold your saucer in your left hand and your teacup in your right.

Ratatouille

As a child I was not very keen on ratatouille. I loved potatoes and meat but ate fish and vegetables only reluctantly. As I grew older and my tastes became more sophisticated, I came to appreciate delicious Provençal vegetables flavoured with Herbs de Provence.

Ratatouille, or *sauté à la niçoise,* as it was first known, is a dish served either hot or cold, that calls for quartered aubergines, onions, courgettes, peppers, and tomatoes as well as herbs and spices. And garlic: no ratatouille is complete without its garlic and olive oil.

The word derives from the Occitan *ratatolha* ("to toss the food"). The dish originated in Nice, though similar versions exist not just throughout the Languedoc region, but also in Spain (*pisto manchego,* often accompanied with a fried egg) and Italy (*caponata*).

There are two schools of thought about how to cook perfect ratatouille. The first insists on all vegetables being cooked together; the other, cooked separately. I like the flavours to mingle, so I follow the first school – browning the onions, adding the peppers, then the courgettes and eggplants; the tomatoes and Herbs de Provence come last. Ratatouilles are infinitely versatile : you may serve them with omelettes, with a little cheese grilled on top, with a fresh basil chiffonade, with olives and capers… Restaurants often serve ratatouille as an accompaniment to grilled meat, but in Provence ratatouille is respected as a course in its own right.

The most famous variation belongs to Michel Guerard (*see MOF*), who first set it out in his book *Cuisine Minceur.* Called *confit byaldi* rather than ratatouille (a pun on the name of a Turkish eggplant meze, *imam bayildi*), it was brought to America by Thomas Keller for the French Kitchen. Keller, serving as a culinary advisor for the Pixar Animation Studios, gave *confit byaldi a* starring role in the movie *Ratatouille*. Far from the rough-cut vegetables most often associated with the dish, the Roma tomatoes, eggplants, and zucchini are cut into thin slices and fanned out like a flower about to open.

It's impossible to watch *Ratatouille* without getting hungry.

Recipe:

Confit byaldi recipe
http://www.nytimes.com/2007/06/13/dining/131rrex.html

Restaurant | Famous Chef:

The French Laundry Cookbook

Red Bull

I came to know Dietrich Mateschitz, the co-founder of this energy drink, during his frequent stays at the Mandarin Oriental in Hong Kong. Red Bull's story is a triumph of savvy marketing.

Red Bull has become the drink of choice for students who need to stay awake all night and adrenaline addicted Wall Street bankers. I myself used to drink it with vodka in my twenties when I wanted to keep going. But Red Bull originated in Thailand as a drink for the working classes; truck drivers drank it to stay awake on long haul journeys.

An Austrian company produces Red Bull, but in Thailand, it is known as called Krating Daeng (which, as you might expect, means Red Buffalo in Thai). On a visit to Thailand in 1984, Dietrich (then marketing director for a toothpaste company), drank his first Krating Daeng, and fell in love with it. He then teamed up with Chaleo Yoovidhya, owner of the Thai brand, to create Red Bull Gmbh.

In France Red Bull was forbidden until 2008; Denmark and Norway continue to ban it, out of concerns for the long-term health effects linked with the drink's high caffeine and taurine levels. (Taurine is a derivative of the amino acid cysteine.) Wild rumours have circulated about Red Bull's mystery ingredients; the more outlandish have accused the company of adding everything from artificial compounds created by rogue American government agencies (glucuronolactone) to actual bull testicles.

The young and trendy mainly mix Red Bull with alcohol, especially vodka, which is contradictory because the two drinks have opposite effects:

Red Bull is a stimulant, whereas alcohol is a depressant. The danger is that the energy drink masks the real effects of the alcohol, and the drinker does not realize his level of intoxication.

Today Red Bull has become one of the major sponsors for Formula One and extreme sports, like wakeboarding, snowboarding, and air racing.

Red Bull gives you wings.

Restaurant | Famous Chef:

Red Bull

http://www.redbullusa.com/cs/Satellite/en_US/

Rolling Stones

Have you ever wondered where the expression *rolling stone* came from? It was during a visit to Val Joanis, a beautiful wine estate in Provence's Côtes du Luberon, near the beautiful little village of Cucuron, that I discovered for myself what 'rolling stones' are. I was able to sift the pebbles (*galet roulé* in French) through my hands and marvel that ordinary looking rocks could have such a profound effect on wine.

Jean Barthelemy Chancel was my guide at Val Joanis. He explained that during the last Ice Age, receding glaciers left behind broad deposits of limestone and stones, which formed soil exceptionally favourable for viticulture. *Galets roulés* are large – each is about the size of a fist – and made of quartzite (metamorphosed sandstone). Over countless millennia, the waters of the Rhône have made them smooth. Most importantly for wine, the stones absorb the sun's heat during the day, releasing it at night, which hastens the ripening of the grapes. The *galets roulés* also act as a protective layer that holds the earth's moisture during the dry summer months.

But is there a connection between my *galets roulés* and the Rolling Stones? The answer is yes: 'rolling stone' was one of the sayings collected by the Dutch Renaissance writer, Desiderius Erasmus, who included it in his *Adagia*, which is essentially a sixteenth century book of quotations. The original reads: *saxum voltum non obducitur musco*. 'A rolling stone collects no moss' – meaning that those who never settle down live happy-go-lucky lives. Muddy Waters used the phrase in his 1948 song "Rollin'

Stone," which gave its name both to the magazine and the rock band.

But despite this somewhat tenuous connection, my friend Sacha Lichine, who owns the Chateau d'Esclans in La Motte promotes his Coq Rouge wine with a song from the Rolling Stones ("Red Rooster"). Chateau d'Esclans produces the world's most expensive rosé, Garrus.

I would be remiss if I did not also mention another Provençal rosé that I love, le Chateau de Selle, which my friend Frédéric Rouzaud makes at the Domaine d'Ott.

The Rolling Stones themselves have their own vineyard in Napa Valley, called Ex Nihilo. They produce a Cabernet blend called Satisfaction; it is made with 66% Cabernet Sauvignon, 19% Merlot, 6% Petit Verdot, 5% Malbec and 4% Petite Syrah with blackberries, black currants, violets and vanilla aroma. They also make Pinot Noir and Riesling ice wines.

Recent studies have suggested that, depending on the music played during a wine tasting, the appreciation of the wine will vary!

Restaurant | Famous Chef:

http://www.val-joanis.com/

Rollmops

I lived in Stockholm for almost a year, and if I had to choose a single memory of Swedish food, it would be the rollmop. During my stay, I opened four outlets at the Berns Hotel, which belonged to the Wallenberg family empire. Opened in 1874, the Berns Hotel is one of Scandinavia's best. In 1998 Peter Wallenberg, (known as "Poker" to his close friends), teamed up with Sir Terence Conran to revamp the Berns' restaurants. As part of Conran restaurants group, I was sent to develop the different concepts: a café, brasserie, fine restaurant, and bar.

A rollmop is a pickled herring wrapped around a green olive, onion or gherkin; a wooden skewer or toothpick holds the roll in place. The rollmop is a standard on many menus in Sweden and throughout Scandinavia. Its origins are German, as its name, though English borrowed the singular form rather than the plural, which is *Rollmopse*. The word 'rollmop' comes from the German words *rollen* ('to roll') and *mops* ('pug dog').

Herring is harvested in the Baltic; before being transported to market, it is gutted, then beheaded and deboned; then it is cured with a special pickling salt to extract water. Afterward the salt is scraped away, and vinegar, sugar, peppercorns, bay leaves, and raw onions are added. My favourite herrings in Sweden were served with mustard and dill.

Pickled herring are traditionally accompanied by sour cream, chopped chives and steamed potatoes. If you're feeling cold, I recommend a glass of akvavit (*see entry*).

For the best Swedish food, go to Östermalms Hallen in Stockholm, the most impressive indoor food market in Scandinavia.

Skall!

Recipe:

Rollmops recipe

http://www.cookitsimply.com/recipe-0010-01270j.html

Restaurants | Famous Chefs:

Berns hotel

http://www.berns.se/

Fredsgatan 12, Danyel Couet, Stockholm

http://www.f12.se/index.php?pageID=135

Salary

What right, you may ask, does the word salary have to its own entry in a book about food? As with *Carat* and *Assassin*, the answer is more than you might expect.

The English word 'salary' derives from the Latin *salarium*, which during the Roman Empire referred to both the tax on salt, and the road by which the salt was transported from its place of production.

You know understand why it is considered bad luck when you accidentally spilled some salt on the table. It is like throwing money through the window.

The French throw a little spilled salt behind them in order to hit the devil in the eye, to temporarily prevent further mischief. In the United States, some people not only toss a pinch of spilled salt over the left shoulder, but crawl under the table and come out the opposite side.

According to *The Oxford Companion to Wine,* the practice of paying workers in wine is older than payments in salt. In Achaemenid Perisa, there are records that relate to the release of wine rations from the city of Shiraz that "amounted to far more than one person could consume: perhaps they would be better described as salaries."

This entry allows me to highlight the injustice propagated within the modern restaurant industry. None of the existing Michelin three-star restaurants could exist without an army of unpaid trainees and apprentices, who are often paid as little as a quarter of the minimum wage; these workers willingly sacrifice themselves to work for the top chefs. I have often seen brigades of forty chefs, almost two-thirds of whom were free labour or on an extremely paltry wage. But unfortunately, high staff numbers are essential for such restaurants to survive; and even under these conditions, wages account for as much as half of an establishment's net expenditures.

Imagine being paid in salt today: how many bags would you be worth? I'd rather be paid in Puligny-Montrachet, myself!

Recipe:

Sea bream baked in salt

http://www.bbc.co.uk/food/recipes/seabreambakedinasalt_92255

Sauerkraut

When I hear the word sauerkraut, I begin thinking of cold midwinter evenings. It is a dish that you associate with a particular season and a particular state of mind. In France, you expect to find this kind of dish in a brasserie, (a type of restaurant that originally meant 'brewery,' as beers were brewed *in situ*). My favourite brasserie is La Brasserie Georges in Lyons. I love its red leather banquettes, marble tables and wooden chairs. La Brasserie is one of the largest in France; it can seat almost 700 guests. Its sauerkraut is exceptional and is served by waiters bearing the dish aloft whilst crossing the restaurant trailing great plumes of steam!

Sauerkraut means 'sour cabbage' in German and is a staple of German and Alsatian cuisine. It is traditionally made by layering shredded cabbage with salt in a crock, pressing it down with a weight and leaving it to ferment. The pressing and the salt draw the liquid out of the cabbage. Meanwhile, naturally occurring lactobacillus bacteria convert the sugars in the cabbage into lactic acid, both giving the sauerkraut its characteristic sour flavour and acting as a preservative.

It is the foundation of the Alsatian dish *choucroute garnie*, where it is simmered with smoked meats and sausages to create a filling winter meal. German immigrants also carried it to America, where it is best loved in the famous Reuben sandwich. Composed of corned beef, sauerkraut, Swiss cheese and Thousand Island dressing, the sandwich is named after Arthur Reuben, owner of Reuben's Delicatessen in New York who is supposed to have created it when the actress Marjorie Rambeau visited the deli at closing time.

Regional variations include Bavarian (with sugar and caraway seeds), and Winekraut, (with white wine). Connoisseurs of Asian cooking will no doubt notice that the preparation is very similar to that of its fiery Korean cousin, kimchee.

Indeed, sauerkraut's origins probably lie in Asia, where the Chinese were pickling cabbage in rice wine by 200 BC; today that dish is known as Chinese *suan cai*. The Mongols under Genghis would use salt instead of wine, and then brought the recipe to Europe where it became popular, especially in Germany. The Dutch would feed sauerkraut to their seamen, as it required no refrigeration, and helped prevent scurvy.

Sauerkraut is thought to have numerous additional health benefits, including improved digestion and cancer prevention. Indeed, sales of the delicacy rocketed in 2005 when a scientific study suggested that it might ward off avian flu.

One of its more bizarre reputed benefits is that drinking its pungent salty juice can cure a hangover.

Perhaps a case of kill or cure?

Recipe:

Sauerkraut recipe by Marco Arbeit

http://www.francechef.tv/recette-choucroute.html

Restaurant | Famous Chef:

Brasserie Georges, Lyons

http://www.brasseriegeorges.com/

Service

The word *service* evokes for me the essence of the hospitality industry. As befitted a bourgeois family, my parents were very strict about manners at our table. My mother constantly referred to the book, *Savoir-Vivre* (*How to Behave!*) by Nadine de Rothschild. The baroness was previously a renowned actress, before marrying Edmond de Rothschild, the banker and owner of storied vineyards (Châteaux Clarke and Malmaison). But don't confuse Nadine with the Baroness Philippine de Rothschild, who inherited Château Mouton Rothschild, Château d'Armailhac and Château Clerc Milon.

I myself first learned about the three types of service in John Cousin and Conrad Tuor's *Wine and Food Handbook*, which I recommend to everyone interested in cuisine. In it, the authors set out gastronomic protocols for every conceivable situation.

Service à *la française* consists of the guest serving himself without restriction. The waiter carries serving dishes in his left hand and offers it to the guest on his left with the serving cutlery facing the diner.

The origin of the English service comes from the Anglo-Saxon tradition, in which the family's head served everyone at the table (see *Knife*). For English service, the waiter presents the dish on his left hand (also on the diner's left), though he himself serves the guest. English service is faster than the French version, but the waiter must be careful that he sets allots food evenly.

Russian service was introduced to France by the diplomat Prince

Alexander Kurakin (1752-1818). This style requires that courses be brought to table in sequential fashion. Kurakin's style was adopted by restaurants, up to the present day.

To sum up, English service consists in the waiter serving the customer; with French service, the customer serves himself; and finally, side-table service (also called *gueridon*), in which the waiter serves the customer from a side-table.

During my time at Lausanne, I sometimes moonlighted as a waiter at the Mövenpick hotel. In Switzerland, service often followed the English style, and as I was then relatively inexperienced, I regret to say that I made rather a few mistakes: pouring sauce into a guest's lap, or failing to distribute food evenly between the diners, so I arrived at the last couple with an empty serving platter.

Choose your style!

Shark's Fin

My friend Claire Nouvian, Ocean Ambassador for the International Union for the Conservation of Nature, and founder of BLOOM, opened my eyes to the overexploitation of our oceans, which represent 70% of the Earth's surface. M*ore than half of the extant shark species are at risk of extinction*, while 100 million are slaughtered each year; in the last fifty years, shark populations have crashed by 90%. Hong Kong is the world's largest importer of shark fins.

Claire is battling bravely against great odds to save the shark, whose fin is considered essential to Cantonese cuisine; its presence on a menu conveys the host's wealth and prestige. Shark's fin belongs to what Chinese regard as '*pu*,' food believed to strengthen and repair the human body. Typically, *pu* is protein rich and easy to digest.

Mainland China's growing middle classes have increased demand for shark's fin. Because the remaining shark meat isn't valued (except for canned dog food), sharks are flung back into the sea without their dorsal fins; unable to swim, they sink to the ocean bottom and die, often eaten by other sharks.

I hope that soon the Hong Kong Hotels Association will promote the prohibition of shark's fin; but only a complete ban is workable, since if one restaurant stops serving shark's fin, business will move to a less scrupulous rival. The shark's fin soup is a must at Chinese weddings, not for its taste, for what it represents: social status.

The largest shark fin seizure in recorded Hong Kong history happened early 2020 with 26 tons of dried shark fins seized from an estimated 38,500 endangered species inside two containers shipped from Ecuador.

'Mastodon' is French slang for something enormous. Like its cousin the mammoth, both animals disappeared as the environment changed, and the first humans arrived in the Americas, hunting them until they were extinct.

Unfortunately, we have not learnt from the past and today there are hundreds of species in danger of extinction because of the greed of the humans: tuna, sea horse, white tiger, many species of shark… Biologists predict that up to 20% of all living populations could become extinct by 2028.

Let us all act before it is too late.

Restaurant | Famous Chef:

Bloom Association

http://www.bloomassociation.org/bloom/abysses-claire-nouvian-en.php

Sidecar & Margarita

Many of the stories I have included in this book have been passed on to me by acquaintances after I've shared with them my passion for culinary history. I first heard the famous Sidecar story from the great professional mixologist Brian van Flandern, whom *Travel & Leisure Magazine* has ranked as one of the top ten bartenders in the world. Van Flandern is renowned for creating cocktails for famed chefs Thomas Keller and Mario Batali in their respective restaurants.

The origin of the Sidecar goes back to World War I in Paris. An American captain who travelled around Paris in a 750cc Clyno sidecar motorbike used to go to his local bar Harry's New York, where the bartender Sam Treadway created this cocktail made of equal parts cognac (brandy), Cointreau and lemon juice. The story goes that Treadway used to drive the officer back to his quarters, transported in his own sidecar.

The recipe then travelled to London, where it was offered at the Buck's Club, where bartender Pat MacGarry became so famous for making Sidecars that he is sometimes credited with inventing it. (MacGarry did invent Bucks Fizz, which is still a popular among the British at brunch.)

By 1930, Harry Craddock listed these variations in his *Savoy's Cocktail Book*: a gin Sidecar was called a White Lady; with vodka, it was a Balalaika.

The Margarita itself is a variation of the Sidecar, with gin replaced by tequila. Van Flandern, who prefers the Don Julio tequila brand, says that there are many stories about how the first Margarita came about. Here are my three favourites:

A bartender called Pancho Morales created the Margarita to honour Rita Hayworth; not yet a star, she was called Margarita Cansino and was working as a dancer in Tijuana.

A second story claims that it was named for one Marjorie King, who was allergic to all alcoholic drinks except for tequila. A bartender named Danny Herrera in Tijuana's Rancho del Gloria Bar named the cocktail after her. For Marjorie, read Margarita.

Finally, the first Margarita may have been created in 1946 at a Christmas pool party thrown by socialite Margarita Sames in Acapulco, Mexico. Margarita mixed drinks behind the bar and asked that her guests to choose the best. The one with three parts tequila, one-part Triple sec and one-part lime was so successful that it then travelled the world bearing her name.

Let's go for a ride!

Recipes:

Sidecar recipe by Eben Freeman

http://www.epicurious.com/video/cocktails/cocktails-classics/1915458821/how-to-make-a-sidecar-cocktail/5295889001

Margarita recipe by Eben Freeman

http://www.epicurious.com/video/cocktails/cocktails-classics/1915458821/how-to-make-a-margarita-cocktail/1915433486

Restaurant | Famous Chef:

Harry's New York Bar, Paris

http://www.harrys-bar.fr

Singapore Sling

On a trip to Singapore, I visited the city's most beautiful landmark, the Raffles Hotel. I loved the colonial colonnades, the courtyard shaded by frangipani trees. There are very few hotels with such character left anywhere. I ended up in the Long Bar, cooled by the wrought iron ceiling fans, peanut shells scattered across the floor crunching underfoot. The star drink of the bar is the Singapore Sling.

The Singapore Sling is composed of gin, cherry brandy, Cointreau, Benedictine, grenadine, pineapple and lemon juices. (The original recipe may also have included club soda, which you will find in other recipes.) It was created by Ngiam Tong Boon for the Long Bar in 1910 based on a traditional sling (gin, vermouth, lemon juice, syrup, angostura bitter and soda). At that time, it was originally called Straits Sling, the local name for Singapore in the old days. It seems that the original drink was amber in colour, rather than the ruby red we know today.

The recipe was tinkered with across the years; the Long Bar's current Singapore Sling was created by Tong Boon's nephew.

At Hong Kong's Mandarin Oriental, we created a cocktail called the Hong Kong Legend after entering a competition that my friend Angie Wong, a journalist with *Time Out* magazine, organized. She wanted a cocktail that was emblematic of Hong Kong. We were one of four whose recipes were featured in *Time Out*.

Andy Wong, our in-house mixologist, created this recipe: a cocktail that contained vodka, *Kuei Hua Cehen Chiew* (Chinese wine), lychee

Singapore Sling

liqueur, lychees, fresh lime juice, simple syrup, and a side order of jelly shots made of vodka, lychees and whiskey. I thought Andy's concoction was the perfect combination for a Cantonese cocktail, as it called for Chinese wine and lychees (a nod to the Mainland) as well as jelly, which required molecular techniques that acknowledged Hong Kong's verve and modernity at that time.

Angie's own creation was called the Wong Island Iced Tea:

Hong Kong Legend

Vodka, Kuei Hua Cehen Chiew, lychee liqueur, lychees, fresh lime juice, simple syrup and a side order of jelly shots made of vodka, lychees and whiskey.

M Bar at the Mandarin Oriental, 5 Connaught Road, Central

Wong Island Iced Tea

Gin, crème de ginger, fresh ginger, orange liquor, grapefruit soda, lime, Hong Kong iced lemon tea.

I wish the Hong Kong Legend the same success as the Singapore Sling!

Recipe:	**Restaurant	Famous Chef:**
Singapore Sling recipe	The Raffles Singapore
http://www.epicurious.com/recipes/drink/views/Singapore-Sling-200060	http://www.raffles.com:80/EN_RA/Property/RHS/

Sot l'y laisse
Chicken Oysters

It is interesting how some expressions have become part of the modern vernacular, and you can find them in any dictionary. The culinary world is no exception, and the expression *sot l'y laisse* is now part of the French language.

We French say: *sot l'y laisse!* , meaning 'only a fool would leave it.' This phrase refers to the soft, tender part of the chicken, tucked just beside the thigh.

My father always says, *"Sot l'y laisse!"* while carving a chicken. He would carefully set aside the two oyster-like pieces found on the back, and keep them separate for our guests, believing that they were the most delicious, tender parts of the entire bird.

One school of thought holds that *sot l'y laisse* refers to the two round pieces of dark meat on the back of the chicken near the thigh. I agree; I never forget to eat the two oysters.

A second school argues that the French expression is third person singular, which means that there can be only *one* piece. These gourmands cite the piece hidden just above the parson's nose (chicken's tail), which is shaped like an ace of spades. The expression means that if you do not take out the uropygial gland from the parson's nose, the yellow part contained in this pocket will give a bad taste to the meat during the cooking. The uropygial gland secretes oil used by the bird for waxing its feathers and making them waterproof. The fool is therefore the person who cooks the bird without extracting the gland!

I have many memories of dining at my grandmother's house as a child; eating roast chicken legs tipped with aluminium foil so I would not burn my fingers. Mamie always gave me the oysters, which I then saved for last.

There are also some nice cuts of beef which are called *pièces du boucher* (butcher cuts) that butchers reputedly keep for themselves rather than sell. These cuts are very tasty and tender: *onglet* (hanger steak), *hampe* (skirt steak) and the extremely tender *bavette* (flank or iron steak).

So, don't be a fool; whatever school you believe in, don't forget these pieces of tender meat!

Recipe:

Chicken oysters with morels recipe

http://www.cookingindex.com/recipes/11778/sot-ly-laisse-aux-morilles-chicken-oysters-with-morels.htm

Spam

Today spam is familiar slang for unsolicited and annoying electronic messages or emails. But originally the word Spam was short for spiced ham, a luncheon meat preternaturally pink in colour and gelatinous in texture, packed in a distinctive rectangular blue and yellow tin.

Minnesota's Hormel Foods first began selling Spam during the Depression. Jay Hormel had a surplus of pork shoulder left over from the production of canned hams, and so created the recipe for canned luncheon meat. Sales were sluggish until the name 'Spam' was suggested, and it was marketed as the 'miracle meat.'

Because it was inexpensive, it quickly became a staple in American homes, helped by Hormel's advertisements including recipes for delicacies such as Spam Ring and Spam Fritters. These recipes included other convenience foods for quick and economical dishes.

Spam's long shelf-life also made it an ideal addition to U.S. Army rations, and during World War II it travelled with American soldiers to become a favourite in places like Hawaii, where it is today enjoyed in a Spam musubi, similar to sushi, and in England, where it was supplied as part of the Lend Lease program, under which the United States supplied food and arms to Allied nations during the war.

Despite its thriving export market, Spam's reputation began to decline after World War II. It was famously lampooned in a 1970s *Monty Python* sketch where a customer in a cafe becomes apoplectic after failing to order a dish that doesn't contain spam. The customer is eventually drowned out by Vikings singing its praises.

Spam

That *Monty Python* sketch is believed to have inspired the term for junk messages and emails but Spam the luncheon meat has survived assaults by comics and food critics; perhaps in response to hard economic times, its sales are thriving. Respected cookery writer Marguerite Patten authored a cookbook devoted to it, and 2020 have a breaking record year boosted by Covid-19 and more people eating at home.

Spam! Spam! Spam! Spam…!

Recipe:

Musubi

Restaurant | Famous Chef:

Marguerite Patten

Steak Tartare | Bistro

In French, the word *Berezina* means 'catastrophe.' It was the name of a river that Napoleon's retreating army crossed in 1812, and where many soldiers died. Later Berezina referred to the entire ill-fated Russian campaign. The few prisoners that Napoleon brought back worked as waiters in the restaurants of Paris. The Russians kept shouting the word *bistro* to each other; it means 'fast' in Russian. The word now refers to small restaurants where you can eat good French food quickly.

Or so I thought. According to the current edition of *Larousse Gastronomique,* the word 'bistro' derives from *bistrouille*, which in northern France meant a brandy mixed with black coffee. Another fairy tale debunked.

But is there a connection between Steak Tartare, a favourite bistro offering, and the Golden Horde, nomads from Central Asia who lived on the southern edges of the Russian Empire? – Again, only the name, it seems.

The Tartars were brilliant horsemen who reputedly could fight for days without ever dismounting. They could sleep on their saddles and would eat on horseback. The Tartars would keep raw meat with some salt (lest the meat spoil) under the saddle, so the very act of riding tenderized the meat. The Steak Tartar was born.

It's a romantic story (if you ignore how sweat would have spoilt the meat), but also an anachronism, since the first Steak Tartar first occurs on a menu in early twentieth century France. In the nineteenth century, it referred to any dish served with Tartar sauce (sour cream and chopped gherkin). Alexandre Dumas mentions 'goat à la tartare' in *The Count of Monte Cristo*, and Honoré de Balzac mentions eel à la tartare.

At Madrid's Estik, which I opened, we specialized in exotic meats: kudu, kangaroo, and ostrich. Our version of steak tartare was prepared à la minute, in a salad bowl, mixing an egg yolk with Dijon mustard, adding salt, pepper, Worcestershire sauce, and Tabasco. We served chopped shallots, capers, gherkins, and parsley in little plates on the side. The meat itself was cut in thin chunks, rather than minced, so that its texture and fibre would be preserved.

The French food historian Patrick Rambourg says that though steak Tartar (originally known as steak à l'Americaine) "only really caught on in the 1950s."

Americans: the Tartars of the twentieth century?

Recipe:	**Restaurant	Famous Chef:**
Gordon Ramsey's Steak Tartare	*A Chef for All Seasons*, 197, 220

Stollen

This festive cake has a medieval pedigree: it is first recorded in the late fourteenth century. Stollen is made from sweet yeast dough with orange and lemon zest; and rum-soaked candied fruit and raisins. A good stollen also includes spices like cardamom, vanilla, and cinnamon. Stollen is also called *Striezel* ('loaf') or *Christollen*, because the bread's shape symbolizes the baby Jesus in swaddling clothes, and it is baked during Advent, the weeks before Christmas.

In Old German the word '*stollen*' meant a city's post or boundary stone, though stollen could also refer to a mine shaft's narrow entrance, which the oblong bread resembles. Dresden, home to Germany's most famous stollen, is near the Erzegebirge Mountains, where silver was first mined around the same time that the first stollen is recorded.

During Advent, once a time of fasting in the Catholic calendar, bakers were forbidden from using milk and butter. The first stollens must have been both tasteless and hard, as the Dresden bakers had to substitute turnip oil to bind the dough. At the behest of those bakers, Prince Elector Ernst (1441-86) wrote a petition to Pope Nicholas V asking that milk and butter be permitted; Nicholas, the same pope who signed a bull permitting slavery of all non-Christians, refused. Callixtus III, Pius II, Paul II, and Sixtus IV also refused to lift the ban.

In 1491, Pope Innocent VIII at last consented in an epistle now famous as the *Butterbrief* ("butter letter"). He agreed that the Saxon bakers might use butter, but only on condition that they pay an annual tax (1/20 of a gold Gulden) for the luxury ingredients: with the proceeds from that tax, Freiburg Cathedral was built.

An average stollen is heavy, at almost 2 kilos. The heaviest on record was served in 1730 by command of August the Strong, Elector of Saxony and King of Poland, for a military review called the Zeithainer Lager (Zeithainer 'Pleasure Dome'). The Stollen baked for this event was so huge that the court architect Mattiäs Daniel Pöppelman had to design a new oven to accommodate it! (Pöppelman also designed Dresden's Zwinger Palace and parts of Dresden Castle.) After baking his stollen for eight days, master baker Johann Andreas Zacharias served up the 1.8-ton behemoth, which needed eight straining horses to move it from oven to table. A carpenter wielding a five-foot long knife portioned the slices out.

Germany's contribution to world cuisine: add stollen to the hamburgers, frankfurters, and sauerkraut!

Recipe:

Stollen recipe

http://www.foodnetwork.com/recipes/saras-secrets/stollen-recipe/index.html

Restaurant | Famous Chef:

Cake Shop, Mandarin Oriental, Hong Kong

http://www.mandarinoriental.com/hongkong/dining/cake_shop/

Swiss Chocolate

During the time I lived in Switzerland, I came to appreciate the Swiss as craftsmen, particularly of watches and chocolate. I am sure that many readers will be familiar with brands like Suchard and Lindt. When I returned to France from Lausanne, I would bring hefty bundles of white milk chocolate Toblerone; Mamie adored chocolates that came in wrappers decorated with idealized Swiss landscapes. Needless to say, my family and friends were always pleased when I came home!

Two major factors helped the Swiss chocolate industry to develop and attain its current dominance. The first factor was a milk surplus in the late nineteenth century. Swiss cows were producing far more milk than the Swiss domestic market could consume; the chocolate industry absorbed the excess by creating solid milk chocolate. The first milk chocolate required condensed milk, which was invented by Henri Nestlé in the early nineteenth century.

The second factor was Rodolphe Lindt's 1879 accidental invention of a method called conching, which allowed chocolate to be mixed evenly with cocoa butter. According to company lore, when Lindt left work for the weekend, he forgot to stop his roller grinder, which went on pressing the cocoa beans for a full three days. When he returned to his factory on Monday morning, he found that the resulting mixture, far from being ruined was silken and smooth. The beans had been pounded and churned to an exquisitely fine texture, resulting in an irresistible velvety chocolate full of subtle aromas. The original machine was a wrought-iron trough fixed to a granite base, with sides that sloped to prevent spills; it resembled a conch shell – hence the name.

Swiss chocolate became famous in the twentieth century not just for its quality, but also for its brand icons. These include Milka, the lilac coloured Simmental cow, (created by Suchard in homage to soprano Milka Ternina). But perhaps Switzerland's most famous chocolate is the Toblerone, whose shape is meant to recall the pyramid-like peak of the Matterhorn. This candy bar's name is an amalgam of the Italian word for nougat (*torrone*) and its creator, who was called Theodor Tobler.

Currently most of these brands are under American corporate ownership: Kraft Foods owns Jacobs, Cote d'Or, Milka, and Cadbury… The only two Swiss major chocolate brands left under domestic ownership are Nestlé and Lindt & Sprüngli.

Tout de bon!

Restaurant | Famous Chef:

Kraft Foods

http://www.kraftfoodscompany.com/Brands/Pages/index.aspx

Table Superstitions

There are many stories about what we should or should not do around a table that could invite bad luck. I have short-listed a few of the stranger traditions.

13 Around the Table

The last Supper of Jesus Christ, twelve apostles and Jesus were present: the superstitious among devout Catholics believe that if there are thirteen around a table, one person will die within a year.

Bread Upside Down

During the Middle Ages, the baker kept the hangman's bread upside down. Today in some devout Italian communities, it is considered sacrilegious to put the bread upside down, since bread is considered to be the body of Christ.

Bread and Butter

When a couple strolling together separate because of an obstacle, the expression 'Bread and Butter' is used as charm to repulse bad luck. Once it has been spread, butter is obviously difficult to separate from bread.

Crossed Knives

It is said that any involuntary representation of the cross is a sign of evil.

Feet on the Table

It is considered bad luck – not to mention bad manners! – to put feet on the table, which can signify that someone has just died or is about to die.

Spilt Salt

According to legend, the apostle Judas Iscariot spilled some salt on the table during the Last Supper, thus indicating his repudiation of Jesus. Leonardo Da Vinci depicted the scene in his representation of the Last Supper of Jesus. It is also possible that the superstition reflects the fact that salt in ancient times was essential; spilling it represented such a waste that it could bring you bad luck.

Tapas

During my six years in Spain I learnt a lot about, and fell in love with, Spanish culture. One of my favourite pastimes was eating tapas with friends on a Sunday in Madrid's La Latina district.

Tapas is an appetizer given free with a drink. But tapas are so much more than food; it is an art of living. Among friends, Spaniards will say *Tapear, ir de tapas o de tapeo*: eating one or two tapas with a drink in a bar; then moving to the next one; and then the next one…

An old friend once related this history of the tapas: in the sixteenth century, Andalucía's inns would serve visitors their famous dry white wine, or sherry, from the Jerez region; each glass would have a piece of bread, *montados de lomo,* or a little plate of meat like chorizo, balanced around its rim to stop flies from hovering or the strong Levante winds from sifting dust inside the glass.

The word *tapas* comes from the Spanish verb *tapear*, which means 'to cover.' Other legends mention the illness of a king who had to drink a glass of wine accompanied with food to reduce (*tapear*) the effect of the alcohol.

My favourite tapas bars are Juana la Loca in the Latina district for its *tortilla de patata* with caramelized onions; and La Castela for *habitas* (green beans with ham) and its fresh grilled seafood *cigalas alla plancha* (grilled Dublin prawns).

I recommend that all my readers *ir de tapas*. Try *jamón ibérico* (*Jabugo* is the world's best ham by far), *tortilla* (an omelette made with potatoes and onions), *croqueta* (potato puree mixed with brunoise of seafood or ham rolled in bread crumbs and then deep-fried), *boquerones* (white anchovies in vinegar), *patatas bravas* (fried potato dices with salsa brava, spicy tomato sauce).

Tapeador…

Recipe:

Tortilla recipe by Ferran Adria

http://www.foodandwine.com/recipes/egg-and-potato-chip-tortilla

Restaurants | Famous Chefs:

Juana la Loca, Madrid

http://www.timeout.com/madrid/madrid/venue/1%3A13287/juana-la-loca

La Castela, Madrid

http://maps.google.com/maps/place?client=safari&rls=en&oe=UTF-8&um=1&ie=UTF-8&q=la+castela+madrid&fb=1&hq=la+castela&hnear=Madrid,+Spain&cid=9221432279364710718&pcsi=9221432279364710718,2

Tapenade

By the end of this book my readers may be tired of Provence, but the region is so beautiful that if you have not yet been, hurry! ... before it becomes as overcrowded and built up as the French Riviera.

Tapenade is typical of southern France. It requires the best black olives, capers, anchovies and a good olive oil. It must be prepared in a mortar to create the perfect paste, which is then spread on toasted bread, fish, pizza, goat cheese, or even boiled eggs.

In Provence, we call it Black Butter, even though it can be green when made with green olives. Its name comes from the Occitan word *tapeno,* or caper, which is an essential ingredient of tapenade.

The original recipe is cited in J.-B Reboul's 1897 classic cookbook, *La cuisinière provençale*. Reboul claimed that one Charles Meynier, chef at Marseilles' Maison Dorée, invented the first tapenade in 1880: 200g black olives; 200g capers; 100g desalted anchovies in filets; 100g marinated tuna; one tablespoon mustard; 200ml olive oil; 5cl brandy or rum; pepper and mixed thyme, rosemary, and oregano.

Modern versions of this recipe play fast and loose with the original: the number of olives has more than doubled, and Patricia Wells cites edgy versions made with green olives, almonds and a little pastis.

One of my first instincts when I arrive in my parents' house in Eygalières is to check fridge to make sure that they have stocked up on tapenade, aioli and anchoiade, the three typical pastes for toasted bread. We eat in the garden while drinking Pastis and listening to the cicadas singing.

Tapenade

A few years back, I came across a great recipe for tomato tart: puff pastry spread with some tapenade, topped with sliced tomatoes and a scattering of anchovies.

Try it for yourself!

Recipe:

Tapenade recipe
http://realnobodyslikeus.typepad.com/real_nobodys_like_us/2009/07/tour-de-french-cuisinestage-3-marseille-to-la-grandemotte.html

Restaurant | Famous Chef:

Le Mas Tourteron, Gordes
http://www.mastourteron.com/uk/index.php

Tarte Tatin

This story is one of my favourites. How a stupid mistake resulted in one of the world's most sublime desserts, just like the waiter who burnt his crêpe; unfazed, he created the Crêpe Suzette.

First let me remind you what a Tarte Tatin is: an apple tart flipped upside down, with apples caramelized in butter and sugar; the mixture is then baked.

In 1898, two sisters, Stéphanie and Caroline Tatin, were running a hotel opposite the Lamotte-Beuvron train station, just south of Orléans. One day Stéphanie forgot about the apples she was cooking for a simple *tarte aux pommes,* when the butter and sugar burned. She tried to hide her mistake by fitting the pastry over the apples; she then flipped it right side up before serving. Her guests were enchanted, and an iconic dessert was born.

Another version of the story has it that one Soeur Tatin dropped the raw tart on her way to the oven. She then cooked it upside down with the apple at the base and the pastry on top.

The Hotel Tatin still stands in Lamotte-Beuvron; delicious tartes are still baked in its wood fired stove. Tatin variants include figs, pineapples, pears, peaches and even tomatoes.

I personally prefer to use puff pastry rather than shortcrust, as I find the puff pastry lighter. I also advise panfrying apples in the caramel on the gas burner before placing the pastry on top; then put your pan directly into the oven. Just make sure that your pan is entirely metal, otherwise you will infuse the smell of burnt plastic into your tart! As a child, I ruined my first Tarte Tatin that way.

Serve the Tarte Tatin warm with vanilla ice cream, or better yet, with a scoop of thick crème fraiche.

Bon appétit!

Recipe:	**Restaurant	Famous Chef:**
Tarte Tatin recipe	Hotel Tatin, Lamotte Beuvron
http://www.telegraph.co.uk/foodanddrink/recipes/7644435/Tarte-Tatin-recipe.html	http://www.hotel-tatin.fr/

Tempura

While living in Hong Kong, my favourite Japanese restaurant was some distance away: in Macao. I loved catching the hydrofoil to visit Tenmasa, which I discovered thanks to my friend Marc Brugger. The chef uses special metal chopsticks which can detect vibrations in the oil. Each slice of vegetable or fish is cooked to perfection.

In 1543 Portuguese sailors first landed on an island south of Kyushu to establish trade with Japan, and to covert the population to Christianity. Portuguese cooks taught their Japanese contacts to fry vegetables and fish; the Japanese not only incorporated the method into their cuisine but improved on it as well.

The word tempura is most often thought to derive from the Latin *tempora*, in reference to *quattuor tempura*, or Ember days, when the church calendar called for fasting and prayers; the devout could eat vegetables and fish, but not meat. A rival etymology would have it that tempura came from the Portuguese word *tempera* ('to season'). A modern Portuguese cousin does exist; it is called *peixinhos da horta*, or garden fish – string beans that when fried look like whitebait or anchovies.

One tempura chef turned writer, Yabuki Isao, claims that the Japanese, who chose the characters (天ぷら) because they *sounded* like the Portuguese word, by chance had appropriate meanings – "gauzy flour," and batter "delicate as negligee"!

In Japan, tempura refers to any meat, seafood or vegetable dipped into a batter and then fried. The Japanese fry chrysanthemum leaves and shiso, shiitake mushrooms and lotus roots, carrots, eggplant as well as white fish, squid, and prawns. The Japanese never use animal fats for deep-frying or sautéing; they use cold-pressed vegetable oils.

Japanese specialist chefs insist that the batter must be both lumpy and delicate as lace. "Techniques have been refined down the centuries. The quality and formula of the oil, its temperature, the formula of the flour for the batter, and the degree of mixing are all important. The timing is so important that it is necessary to sit immediately in front of the chef for the best results."

The oil's temperature is therefore strictly kept at around 170C°, and the batter never left to stand; a chef will cook it in small batches.

Tempura is served with a clear dipping sauce (*tentsuyu*), to which a diner will add grated daikon and ginger, which help in the digestion of oily foods.

Better than fish and chips!

Recipe:

Tempura recipe

http://www.foodnetwork.com/recipes/vegetable-tempura-recipe/index.html

Restaurant | Famous Chef:

Tenmasa, Altira hotel, Macau

http://www.altiramacau.com/eng/restaurantsbars_1_3.php

Thousand-Year-Old Egg

Eating a thousand-year-old egg (*pidan*) was one of my first culinary experiences after moving to Hong Kong. I ordered the dish at Lei Gardens, one of the city's best Cantonese restaurants. When I saw the egg, its yolk a dark green and the white a dark brown, and when I smelled sulphur and ammonia, I felt a little squeamish, so I ate the delicacy gingerly. The taste, however, surprised me: it was very good. It had an earthy, ashen, sour taste, with a very unique texture – a vinegary blackened yolk encased in solidified jelly.

The thousand-year-old egg is actually younger than its name; a Chinese urban myth dates its creation to the late Ming dynasty. A Hunanese farmer found an abandoned duck's nest whose eggs had been left in a pool of slaked lime that months before he had used for his house's mortar and plaster. If the story is true, you have to wonder about the farmer: he was either foolhardy or very hungry to taste the eggs, since calcium hydroxide (the chemical name for slaked lime) has side-effects rather more unpleasant than heartburn: it can cause the skin to blister and the eyes to burn, even in small amounts. But he was lucky; the accident had delicious results. He decided that for perfection his eggs needed only a little salt.

To make *pidan*, the Chinese use salt and an alkaline substance, most often sodium carbonate, wood ash, lime or lye. Tea may sometimes be added for flavour, and mud to protect the egg while it matures; the process

Thousand-Year-Old Egg

may take from one to six months. Harold McGee describes this as "an inorganic version of fermentation… it breaks down some of the complex, flavourless proteins and fats into simpler, highly flavourful components."

In Thailand this egg has a rather less appetizing name: it is called "horse urine egg," due its strong odour of ammonia.

I think it needs to be rebranded.

Recipe:

Thousand Year Old Egg recipe

http://www.recipesource.com/ethnic/asia/chinese/preserved-duck-eggs1.html

Restaurant | Famous Chef:

Lei Garden, Hong Kong

http://www.leigarden.hk/English/local_detail.asp?id=0885986E-E3CF-4E16-8CEA-927FFDB812B6

Toque Blanche

I first wore a toque while studying at Lausanne. I have to say that I am not a hat person: anything you put on my head does me no favours. But despite my antipathy for hats, I will always remember my first day in a chef's uniform, complete with white toque, white jacket, blue and white checked trousers, white apron, clogs and, finally, the neckerchief.

For me, toque blanche ('white hat') sets the Grands Chefs apart from mere cooks. When on my seventh birthday Paul Bocuse stopped by my family's table at L'Auberge du Pont de Collonges, I was really impressed by his tall figure, so immaculate with the hundred-pleated white hat.

The word *toque* originates with Arabic (the original word was *taqa*, 'opening'). During the Middle Ages, a toque was the symbol of artisans; each specialist had its own unique style: the butcher's was distinct from the baker's.

My friend Gilles Bragard, famous for being the Christian Dior of Chefware (see *C.C.C.*) offers toques in a variety of styles: some are disposable; others are of varying heights; in addition to the *Douga* (skull cap), you may find the *Goyan*, the *Khani* and the *Milon* chef's hat. The skull cap (called *calotte* in French) is currently quite trendy. You might also have heard as well of the *charlotte*, which is mainly used by pastry chefs. The Chef's toque must be of a unique shape to distinguish the Grand Chef from the rest of the brigade.

The toque blanche was designed out of hygiene considerations: its white shade makes the smallest speck of dirt stand out, so it is easy to clean. The toque keeps the chef's hair out of the food and keeps grease out of the hair. In addition, the rim absorbs the chef's sweat, while both the hat's height and the holes on top encourage the free flow of air – an important feature in a hot kitchen.

Finally, the toque's pleats (which supposedly represent the hundred possible ways to cook an egg) allow the hat to fold up easily.

OUI, CHEF…!

Restaurant | Famous Ches:

L'École Hotelière de Lausanne

http://www.ehl.edu/eng

Trou Normand

This expression is very hard to understand unless you are French or a gourmet connoisseur. The literal translation is "Norman hole." It refers to the custom in Normandy of having a glass of Calvados, the local apple eau-de-vie (see *Alcohol*), between two courses.

In the French countryside, meals can last for hours; a profusion of food is served. To help digestion, diners have a glass of Calvados between courses to 'make a hole' in the food they have eaten, thereby bringing back the appetite. Besides, with its high level of alcohol, Calvados was believed to have anti-bacterial qualities, which protect against indigestion from dishes like *le plateau de fruits de mer*.

In modern restaurants, Calvados is usually served as a refreshing sorbet. For a degustation menu of more than six courses, you will be served a sorbet or a granita after the third or fourth course to cleanse your palate before the entrees resume.

I have also come across the Trou Provençal, which works on the same principle, though with *marc de Provence* instead of Calvados. But in case you don't like strong alcohol, you can always cleanse your palate with a rosemary granita or sorbet.

Granita is recorded during the reign of the infamous Roman emperor Nero, whose servants would climb the Apennine Mountains to collect snows that they would later mix with "fruit pulps, flower petals, honey and wines for his banquets. The exact ingredients and proportions were kept secret – the 'little grains' were to be enjoyed only in royal circles.' Later,

Sicilians would turn mountain snows into a confection out of crushed ice, lemon and sugar; it was the more refined ancestor of the American snow cone. Today fruit syrups are used for the confection.

The sorbet is slightly different, in that it is made with water and fruit juices, or sometimes even with wine and liquor. Its texture is smoother, though it should not be confused with sherbet, which contains a very small amount of cream. Finally, ice cream, as you might guess from its name, is made with still more milk or cream, and has a very smooth texture.

The next time you have a big meal, don't forget to dig yourself a hole!

Recipe:

Trou Normand recipe

http://halby-herald.blogspot.com/2007/11/recipe-trou-normand-apple-sorbet-with.html

Turkey

Turkey features on most holiday menus, not just in the United States but in Europe as well. I have to confess that in my family we were not very keen on the bird; we preferred game, which was fortunate, since Christmas comes right in the middle of the hunting season.

But have you ever wondered why a bird carries the name of a country? The turkey is native to North America; for many years it was confused with the guinea fowl. It was originally imported by Turkish merchants; so the French began calling it *coq d'Inde* which became 'dinde' and then 'dindon.' The Italian know it as *galle d'India*, the Germans *indianische Henn*, and the Swedes as *Kalkon*, in reference to the Indian city of Calcutta where Vasco da Gama first landed. The confusion came about because for centuries the Americas were called 'The New Indies.'

So next Christmas show off your culinary knowledge by telling everybody that there are mistaken in calling the bird they are eating a turkey, and that the right word should be *Meleagris gallopavo* (Latin) or *uexolotl* (from Nahuatl, the language of the Aztecs).

Here is a recipe you can try as well: Turkducken: a de-boned turkey stuffed with a de-boned duck stuffed with a de-boned chicken.

This technique comes courtesy of Vera Goodwine, one of Hong Kong's most famous hostesses. She has fed as many as twenty-eight people with that particular dish!

Happy Turkey Day!

Recipe:

Turducken recipe

http://homecooking.about.com/od/turkeyrecipes/ss/turduckensbs.htm

Turkish Delight

Turkish Delight, as it is known in England, reminds me of my first trip to Marrakech, the Red City, where I stayed with a group of friends in a *ryad*, a house with an enclosed courtyard and garden (*ryad* means "garden" in Arabic). We were in the middle of the ancient city's medina, a labyrinth of shaded alleys where merchants keep their fascinating stalls…

The real name of Turkish Delight is *rahat lokum*, meaning "respite for the throat" in Arabic. *Lokum* is sticky jelly made by cooking syrup with corn starch and cream of Tartar (potassium bitartrate); once the mixture has set, it is rolled in icing sugar and diced into cubes. Turkish Delight may taste of lemons, oranges, roses, chocolate, vanilla, or *crème de menthe*. (Other, less orthodox flavours include clotted cream!) Pistachio, hazelnut or walnuts may be sprinkled on top.

Most children will have come across Turkish Delight not in any candy store, but rather in C. S. Lewis' *Narnia* books, where a wicked queen uses it as a bribe to tempt a boy into treachery. "Each piece was sweet and light to the very centre and Edmund had never tasted anything more delicious… It was enchanted Turkish Delight and anyone who had once tasted it would want more and more of it, and would even, if they were allowed, go on eating it until they killed themselves…"

Turkish Delight was invented in 1777 by the confectioner Bekir Effendi, who had moved from Kastamonu on the Black Sea coast and settled in Istanbul. He opened a tiny shop in what was then the capital's business district (Bahcekapi – now known as Istanbul's old quarter), where he sold traditional sweets from his native Anatolia. The ancestor of *lokum* was created from honey or grape molasses (*pekmez*) bound with flour. By substituting sugar and corn starch, Bekir Effendi created the first Turkish Delight. His descendants (the fourth and fifth generations) still run the shop he opened on Hamidiye Caddesi.

Lokum was brought back to England by a nineteenth century traveller returning from Istanbul: hence Turkish Delight!

What, no English Delight?

Recipe:

Turkish delight recipe

http://thefoody.com/sweets/turkishdelight.html

Valentine's Chocolate

I have never been a great fan of Valentine's Day, as I hate to be forced to do something just because everybody else is doing it. If you want to have a romantic dinner with your beloved, or offer her flowers, you shouldn't do it just because the calendar dictates.

Valentine's Day has its origins in the ancient Roman celebration of Lupercalia. Held on the Ides of February (15 February), which marked the beginning of spring, Lupercalia honoured the woodland gods Lupercus and Faunus. Lupercalian festivities included the pairing of young women and men. An eligible man would draw the name of an unattached woman (written on a clay tablet) from an earthen jar, and each couple would be paired together until next year's celebration. The festival was banned by Pope Gelasius in the late fifth century and replaced by the Feast of Saint Valentine.

The saint's reputation as the patron of lovers, though, was a later invention of the English poet Geoffrey Chaucer in his *Parlement of Foules*. The story goes that Valentine, who was a priest with a romantic heart, married couples in defiance of an imperial edict that Roman soldiers had to remain bachelors. When his defiance was discovered, Valentine was put to death on 14 February.

But the association of chocolate and Valentine's Day was more recent still: it was a spectacularly successful marketing ploy by the English confectionary firm Cadburys. According to *The Cambridge World History of Food*, it was Cadburys which "first emphasized the connection between boxes of chocolate and romance. Chocolates and cut flowers became tokens of romantic love and soon were the typical presents given to a woman."

Valentine's Day continues to evolve in unexpected ways. In Japan, for instance, it is customary for women to offer chocolate to their male colleagues; this candy is called *chō-giri choko* ('obligatory chocolate') whereas sweets bought for a loved one is *honmei-choko*, ('favourite chocolate'). Meanwhile, the men are supposed to reciprocate on White Day, by offering a gift around three times the value.

Still looking for my Valentine's!

Restaurant | Famous Chef:

Bernachon chocolatier, Lyons

http://www.bernachon.com/accueil_en.html

Vatel & Chantilly

Today Vatel is a prominent hotel school run by my friend Karine Benzazon, whose father Alain Sebban is the president and founder. There are fifty schools around the world; Institut Vatel is ranked first in Europe, though as an alumnus of Lausanne, I'm not sure about that!

What is the relation between a château in the Loire Valley and François Vatel, the renowned chef who habitually organized splendid banquets for as many as 2000 guests back in the seventeenth century?

Vatel was known for his perfectionism and for creating the first crème Chantilly in 1671, during one of his renowned banquets; though made in honour of Louis XIV, the dessert was named after the château de Chantilly. Crème Chantilly unites whipped cream, a little bit of icing sugar and some vanilla essence.

But Vatel is also famous for killing himself during that same banquet. He was a perfectionist, and on the evening before he died, two tables went without roast meat – as a few latecomers had joined the party unexpectedly – and fog ruined the launch of an expensive firework display. Vatel felt humiliated and could not sleep.

In the kitchens before dawn the next day, Vatel met his fishmonger, who apologized that only two loads of fish were coming – the fishmonger did not realize that Vatel had sent to all the ports for supplies.

Vatel felt he had lost his honour and reputation. He returned to his room and fell on his own sword. His body was discovered by staff coming to tell him that the fish had finally arrived.

The death of Francois Vatel has been by the Marquise de Sévigné in her correspondence with her daughter, the Marquise de Grignan: *"Night falls. The fireworks fail, because of a fog over everything; they had cost sixteen thousand francs. At 4:00 AM Vatel was everywhere, but he found everyone asleep; he ran into a small purveyor who brought him only two loads of fish; Vatel asked him, "Is that all?" He answered, "Yes, sir." He didn't know that Vatel had sent to all the ports. Vatel waited a while; the other purveyors didn't come; his head felt hot, he thought that he would have no other fish; he found Gourville, and said to him: "Sir, I will not survive this disgrace; I have honour and a reputation to lose." Gourville laughed at him. Vatel went up to his room, stood his sword against the door, and passed it through his heart; but that was only at the third stab, for the first two weren't fatal: he fell dead. However, the fish started coming from every direction; they looked for Vatel to distribute them; they went to his room, they started banging, they broke down the door; they found him drowned in his blood; they ran to the Prince, who was in despair…"*

Recipe:

Chantilly recipe

http://www.cuisine-french.com/cgi/mdc/l/en/recettes/creme_chantilly.html

Restaurant | Famous Chef:

Vatel International Business School

http://www.vatel.fr/V3/index.php

WELLINGTON

For me, *boeuf en croûte* is synonymous with Sunday family gatherings with my grandparents, uncles, aunts, and cousins, either at our house or at an uncle's. It was only when I arrived in England during the summer of 1997 that I realized the British had their own version, called Beef Wellington.

Arthur Wellesley, the first duke of Wellington, is primarily famous for his 1815 victory at Waterloo in Belgium. Every Frenchman arriving from Paris by train used to pass through Waterloo Station, which is as good a sign as any of the acerbic British sense of humour.

But the Duke also lent his name to a town in the English county of Somerset, the capital of New Zealand, a pair of boots and a recipe. Not bad going for one person.

Although no gourmet, the Duke loved a dish made of beef tenderloin coated with foie gras and mushroom *duxelle*, folded in puff pastry and then baked.

The French say that this most British of entrees has its origins as *fillet en croûte*, and joke that the English version resembles the Duke's shiny Hessian boots. In fact, the Duke of Wellington asked his shoemaker on St. James' Street to shorten his Hessian boots. The shoemaker obliged: he also removed the boots' shafts so that they would better fit around the leg. The boots – also called 'Wellies' – still carry the duke's name.

So, shall we name dishes after moccasins, brogues, slippers, stilettos, and espadrilles?

Beef Flip Flop, please!

Recipe:

Gordon Ramsay's recipe

Restaurant | Famous Chef:

http://www.bbcgoodfood.com/recipes/2538/beef-wellington

Winebottle Trivia

As a boy, I often wondered why bottles for red wine were tinted green, while bottles for white wines were often transparent. By the way, in case you're wondering, I asked that question when I was completely sober!

Men have made wine since ancient times: Jancis Robinson makes the slightly (to my way of thinking) irreverent point that "apes often seek out fermenting fruits… Given the behaviour of apes, winemaking is at least as old as humanity itself…"

So why are red wine bottles made only of dark tinted glass? The answer resides with tannin, the bitter polyphenol present in grape skins, seeds, and the wood of the barrels where wine is aged. (Tannins are present in higher quantities in red wine than in white.) Tannins dissolve with time, a process which both clarifies the wine and improves its taste as it ages; however, they deteriorate when exposed to light, hence the use of green glass which filters out destructive UV rays.

A standard bottle of wine is normally 750ml but depending on its content the bottle's name may change, using the proper names of Biblical kings. For a bottle of Burgundy or Champagne, the names and sizes are as follows: Jéroboam (3 litres); Rehoboam (4.5litres); Methuselah (6 litres); Salmanazar (9 litres); Balthazar (12 litres); Nebuchadnezzar (15 litres); Melchior (18 litres); and Solomon (20 litres). Confusingly, bottles of Bordeaux share some of these names, though the volumes differ: the Marie-Jeanne; the double magnum (3 litres); the Jéroboam (4.5 litres); and finally, the Impériale. These larger bottles are much sought after by connoisseurs of Bordeaux, as the larger size bottles (called 'formats') "favour slow but subtle wine ageing."

Both red and white wine bottles use corks, despite the current mania for screwcaps. Cork is made from the bark of a certain oak, which is chosen for its non-permeability, elasticity and fire resistance.

A final characteristic of wine bottles is the rounded bottom, often referred to as a 'punt.' Its concave shape allows bottles to be stacked together with ease; the punt also allows a place to hook the thumb when pouring; for sediments to collect; or to balance the bottle on uneven surfaces. The design is especially useful in France, when you want to balance a bottle on gravel while you're busy playing *boules*.

Anyone for Rosé?

You Are What You Eat

These hundred stories mark my evolution from the son of a line of jewellers to a passionate gourmet.

It was thanks to my encounters with talented chefs that the world of five senses opened up for me; there have been a thousand and one discoveries, with more, I hope, to come. I must mention in particular Andoni Aduriz, Ferran Adria, Oriol Balaguer, Martin Berasategui, Raymond Blanc, Heston Blumenthal, Daniel Boulud, George Blanc, Michel Bras, la Mère Brazier, Antonio Carluccio, Pierre Gagnaire, Thomas Keller, Virgilio Martinez, Sam Mason, Joël Robuchon, and Jordi Roca. My most profound gratitude, however, is for Monsieur Paul, who was the prime mover and inspiration for the direction my life has taken.

I hope that, after years of eating good meals and drinking good wines, and after living and working in every sort of restaurant in eleven different countries, I have been able to offer you a few interesting facts and relate a few urban legends that amused you. I hope that you will now entertain your own guests with these stories; may *The Curious Gourmand* spark passionate debates around your table!

If you have food stories to share with me, or questions about food history to ask, please write me at my e-mail address:

ambmelon@gmail.com

I hope that you will share this book with your friends, colleagues, and family members.

Once again, I would like to thank my grandmother, Petite Mamie, for inspiring me; my parents, Pierre et Christiane, for giving me the opportunity to fulfil my dream; and my friends who have encouraged me from the beginning to write this book. Many thanks also to the friends and colleagues who have shared their stories.

Dear readers, I hope to see you very soon for another chapter! Meanwhile, remain curious, and be adventurous…

Yours,

Antoine Melon

Bibliography

INTRODUCTION

For a modern interpretation of the Floating Island, try Béatrice Peltre's blog La Tartine Gourmande (12 December, 2007):

http://www.latartinegourmande.com/2007/12/12/vanilla-cardamom-snow-eggs/

Peltre also has a very good discussion of the difference between Floating Islands and Snow Eggs.

APICIUS

Harold McGee includes a few anecdotes about this tragic hero (to my way of thinking) and his menus in *On Food and Cooking: The Science and Lore of the Kitchen*, Scribner, 2004.

BAIN MARIE

Jordi Roca discusses his book *La Cocina al Vacio (Sous-Vide Cuisine)* in this *Art Culinaire* interview, "Five Days in Barcelona (and Points North)," 22 September 2006.

BARBECUE

John Thorne's *Serious Pig: An American Cook in Search of His Roots* provides an excellent narrative of the origins of the *barbacòa*. North Point Press, Farrar Straus Giroux, 1996.

BOCUSE D'OR

This entry is taken from *Knives at Dawn*, Andrew Friedman's detailed account of the US team's experience in 2008. Free Press, December 2009. Geir Skeie, the 2008 gold medalist, has also published an autobiographical cookbook, which includes a simplified recipe for his winning Bocuse d'Or menus.

BOUCHON

For an English assessment of my hometown's *bouchons*, see Barbara Bradlyn Morris in *The Washington Post*, 29 August, 2004.

http://www.washingtonpost.com/wp-dyn/articles/A38867-2004Aug27.html

Also, Roy Furchgott in "In Lyon, Battle of the Bouchons," 2 September 2001

http://www.washingtonpost.com/wp-dyn/content/article/2001/09/02/AR2005041402500.html

For an older, but comprehensive look at Lyons' bouchons, read Steven Greenhouse in *The New York Times*, 26 August 1990, "What's Doing in Lyons." I also liked R. W. Apple Junior's article in Saveur #23 http://www.saveur.com/article/Travels/The-Bouchons-of-Lyon

CHATEAUX OF BORDEAUX

I owe Kathleen Buckley for this entry, and encourage my readers to follow her at *Wine Enthusiast Magazine*. I also find the Wine Doctor a useful – and funny – website.

CHILIES

For a very funny account of how chilies affect our bodies, see "A Perk of Our Evolution: Pleasure in Pain of Chilies," The New York Times, 20 September 2010.

COCIDO

For regional variations and a cultural history of Madrid's cocido, see the entry in *The Oxford Companion to Food*.

CROISSANT

People love to argue about the croissant almost as much as they love to eat it! See Harold McGee for the history of my favorite breakfast pastry and also an analysis of the process that makes them so delicious. *On Food and Cooking*, page 567.

DAUBE OF BEEF

Patricia Wells. *At Home in Provence: Recipes Inspired by Her Farmhouse in France*. Scribner, 1996, page 263.

DIM SUM

Margaret Leeming and Man-Hui May Huang give an interesting account of the history of Chinese snacks in *Dim Sum: Chinese Light Meals, Pastries, and Delicacies*. Macdonald Books. 1985. See Martin Yan for modern interpretations of dim sum.

FORK

For readers interested in learning more about the evolution of the fork, I recommend *Feeding Desire: Design and the Tools of the Table: 1500-2005*, Assouline Publishing 2006. Many of this entry's details are taken from this book's collection of essays. For the story of Teodora Ducas, see page 108ff; for snide remarks about Henri III, see page 111; for Louis XIV eating with his hands, see pages 46 and 122. For the fork's progress through Europe, see page 108 note 15.

GAZPACHO

The New York Times has an interesting survey of gazpacho's history: "Through Andalucia, in Search of Gazpacho," Andrew Ferren, 4 September, 2005.

HONEYMOON

"Wild Honey With and Without Locusts, or, The Inconclusive History of the Word Honeymoon," Anatoly Liberman, Oxford University Press

USA Blog, 12 March 2008

http://blog.oup.com/2008/03/honeymoon/

KARCADE

John Feeney writes about the origins and cultural background of this drink in "The Red Tea of Egypt," *Saudi Aramco World*, September/ October 2001.

KNIFE LORE

The quote is from *Feeding Desire: Design and the Tools of the Table 1500-2005*, Assouline Publishing, 2006, "The Sexual Politics of Cutlery," page 112.

LAGUIOLE

The New York Times has an interesting article on Michel Bras' cutlery: Florence Fabricant, "French Chef Reaches for a Knife and Finds It In Japan" 28 September, 2005.

MELON

For the stories of melons (the plants, not my relations!), see the entry in *The Cambridge World History of Food*. CUP, 2000, page 1813.

MOF

For details on a recent competition, see Jancis Robinson's amusing blog entry, "The Battle for the Initials MOF," 24 March 2007.

MORUE

The blog "French Virtual Café" has a good description of this dish's history, as well as recommendations for restaurants in America which serve delicious *brandade de morue!*

http://frenchvirtualcafe.blogspot.com/2009/07/brandade-de-morue-de-nimes.html

NOTE A NOTE

Hervé This discusses technology and food in the 19 January 2010 edition of *The New Scientist*. Also, This and Pierre Gagnaire are not the only chefs who object to the 'molecular' label: in this *Guardian* interview, Heston Blumenthal also dismisses it: "Molecular Gastronomy Is Dead,"

http://observer.guardian.co.uk/foodmonthly/futureoffood/story/0,,1969722,00.html

PACOJET

To read more about the strange history of this appliance, see "A Short History of the Pacojet (as told to me by Gunter Scheible)," 16 July 2009:

http://happypacojetting.blogspot.com/2009/07/short-history-of-pacojet-as-told-to-me.html

PAELLA

The quotes come from *The Dean & Deluca Cookbook*. Ebury Press, 1996, pages 229-30.

PERSONALITIES

My primary source for this entry is Conrad Tuor's indispensable *Wine and Food Handbook*, which was a set text during my years as a student at Lausanne. I highly recommend the updated version.

PIZZA

For a good overview of the origins of pizza, see Evelyne Slomon's *The Pizza Book: Everything There Is To Know About the World's Greatest Pie*, Times Books, 1984.

POMODORO

The Cambridge World History of Food, vol. 1; II.C. Important Vegetable Supplements; "Tomatoes" Janet Long, p. 351-8; CUP; 2000.

POPCORN

For an account of the origins of modern corn, see Joan Peterson in *Repast: Quarterly Newsletter of the Culinary Historians of Ann Arbor*, volume XIX, Number 2, Spring 2003. "Maize: Mexico's Gift to the World," pages 4-6.

http://cooks.aadl.org/files/cooks/repast/2003_Spring.pdf

Betty Fussell also has a comprehensive account in *The Story of Corn*, The University of New Mexico Press, 2004. For a discussion of popcorn in the molecular kitchen, see "Daily Dish," in the *Los Angeles Times* Blog, 1 April 2009: "No More Dragon's Breath at the Bazaar?" Also, see Harold McGee for the chemistry of the exploding kernel.

PURÉE DE POMMES DE TERRE

For Robuchon's tips on the best mashed potatoes, see *The Complete Robuchon*. Knopf, 2008, page 622ff.

RATATOUILLE

For those readers who want to make the Pixar dish at home, see Thomas Keller's *French Laundry Cookbook*, pages 178-9.

RED BULL

For a collection – and refutation – of the many urban myths (including the claim that Red Bull contains a government-manufactured stimulant) and Internet stories that have grown up around Red Bull, see Barbara Mikkelson on Snopes.Com:

http://www.snopes.com/medical/potables/redbull.asp

For the brand strategies that brought about the drink's success, see Kenneth Hein in *Brandweek*, 28 May 2001: "A Bull's Market – the marketing of Red Bull Energy Drink."

SALT

For an on-line analysis of the connection between "salt" and "salarium," try the discussion at Yahoo Answers:

http://answers.yahoo.com/question/index?qid=20100306124429AAUk7v5

Details on salaries paid in wine come from Jancis Robinson's *The Oxford Companion to Wine*, page 604.

STEAK TARTARE

For a debunking of the myth that Steak Tartare originated with the Mongols of Central Asia, see Craig S. Smith in *The New York Times*, 6 April 2005: "The Raw Truth: Don't Blame the Mongols (or Their Horses)":

http://www.nytimes.com/2005/04/06/dining/06steak.html?pagewanted=print&position

STOLLEN

The Dresden Stollen Festival has its own website, which includes many fascinating details about Friedrich Augustus' festival in 1730:

http://www.stollenfest.com/history.php

SWISS CHOCOLATE

For an involved account of the discovery of the conching process, see *Chocolate Wars: From Cadbury to Kraft: 200 Years of Sweet Success and Bitter Rivalry*, pages 98-100; Deborah Cadbury; Harper Press, 2010.

THOUSAND YEAR OLD EGG

Harold McGee, *On Food and Cooking*, pages 116-17.

TROU NORMAND

For an account of granita's origins, see Nadia Roden's *Granita Magic*. Artisan Press, 2003, page 13.

TURKISH DELIGHT

The Candyblog discusses the myths and history surrounding this sweet in a post on 13 December, 2005:

http://www.candyblog.net/blog/item/candy_essay_turkish_delight/

WINEBOTTLE TRIVIA

See Jancis Robinson, *The Oxford Companion to Wine*, page 499 – (on the origins of viticulture), and 96-9 (on bottle formats). See also Pam Belluck in the New York *Times* for archaeological finds involving winemaking operations dated over 6000 years ago: "Cave Drops Hints to Earliest Glass of Red," 11 January, 2011.

General Bibliography

Accademia Italiana della Cucina. *La Cucina: The Regional Cooking of Italy.* Jay Hyams, translator. Rizzoli Publications, 2009.

Allen, Stewart Lee. *In the Devil's Garden: A History of Forbidden Fruit.* Ballantine, 2003.

The Art of Home Cooking. Leonard Moreton & Company. The Stork Cookery Service. 1963.

Bishop, George. *The Booze Reader: A Soggy Saga of a Man in His Cups.* Sherbourne Press. 1965.

Bras, Michel. *Essential Cuisine.* Ici La Press. 2002.

Cadbury, Deborah. *Chocolate Wars: From Cadbury to Kraft: 200 Years of Sweet Success and Bitter Rivalry.* Harper Press, 2010.

Charpentier, Henri. *Being the Memories of Henri Charpentier.* The Modern Library, Random House, 2001.

Clark, Sam and Sam. *Casa Moro: The Second Cookbook.* Ebury Press, 2004.

Coates, Clive. *Grands Vins: The Finest Chateaux of Bordeaux and their Wines.* University of California Press, 1995.

Coffin, Sarah, "Historical Overview" in *Feeding Desire: Design and the Tools of the Table* 1500-2005, Assouline Publishing, 2006.

Conran, Terence, Hopkinson, Simon, and Harris, Matthew. *The Bibendum Cookbook.* Conran Octopus, 2008.

Davidson, Alan, editor. *The Oxford Companion to Food,* Oxford University

Press, 2006.

Drachenfels, Suzanne von, "The Design of Table Tools and the Effect of Form on Etiquette and Table Setting," in *Feeding Desire: Design and the Tools of the Table: 1500-2005*, Assouline Publishing 2006.

Ferniot, Jean, *French Regional Cooking*. 1991. Crescent Books.

Friedman, Andrew. *Knives at Dawn*. Free Press, 2009.

Fussell, Betty: *The Story of Corn*. University of New Mexico Press. 2004.

Glanville, Philippa, "Manufacturing and Marketing in Europe, 1600-2000," in *Feeding Desire: Design and the Tools of the Table*: 1500-2005, Assouline Publishing 2006.

Goldsborough, Jennifer, "The Proliferation of Cutlery and Flatware Designs in 19th Century America," in *Feeding Desire: Design and the Tools of the Table: 1500-2005*, Assouline Publishing 2006.

Goldstein, Dara, *Implements of Eating, in Feeding Desire: Design and the Tools of the Table: 1500-2005*, Assouline Publishing, 2006.

Keller, Thomas. *The French Laundry Cookbook*. Workman Publishing, 1999.

Landen, Dinsdale, and Daniel, Jennifer. T*he True Story of H. P. Sauce*. Methuen, 1985.

Larousse Gastronomique. Hamlyn, 2009.

Leith, Prue, & Waldegrave, Caroline. *Leith's Cookery Bible. Bloomsbury*. 1996.

Leeming, Margaret, and Man-Hui May Huang, *Dim Sum: Chinese Light Meals, Pastries, and Delicacies*. Macdonald Books. 1985.

Lo, Kenneth. *New Chinese Cookery Course*. Macdonald Books. 1985.

Lupton, Ellen, "Modern Flatware and the Design of Lifestyle," in *Feeding Desire: Design and the Tools of the Table: 1500-2005*, Assouline Publishing 2006

McGee, Harold, *The Science and Lore of the Kitchen*, Scribner, 2004.

Patten, Marguerite. *Spam the Cookbook*. Hamlyn, 2009.

Peterson, Joan. "Maize: Mexico's Gift to the World," in Repast: Quarterly

Newsletter of the Culinary Historians of Ann Arbor. Volume 19, Number 2, pages 3-6. Spring 2003.

Proust, Marcel. *Remembrance of Things Past*. Terence Kilmartin, translator. Penguin, 1981.

Robinson, Jancis. *The Oxford Companion to Wine*, Oxford University Press, 2006.

Robuchon, Joël. *The Complete Robuchon*. Knopf, 2008.

Roden, Nadia. *Granita Magic*. Artisan Press, 2003.

De Sévigné, Madame. *Selected Letters*. Longman, 2003. Pages 97-99.

Skeie, Geir. *World Champion from Childhood to the Bocuse d'Or*. Skeie Metro Forlag. 2009.

Soltner, André. *The Lutèce Cookbook*. Knopf, 1995.

Slomon, Evelyne, *The Pizza Book: Everything There Is To Know About the World's Greatest Pie*. Times Books, 1984.

Tannahill, Reay: *Food in History*, Broadway, 1995.

Thompson, David. *Thai Food*. Viking, 2002.

Thorne, John, with Matt Lewis Thorne. *Serious Pig: An American Cook in Search of His Roots*. North Point Press, Farrar Straus Giroux, 1996.

Tschirky, Oscar. *The Cook Book by 'Oscar' of the Waldorf*. General Books, 2010.

Tuor, Conrad and Cousins, John. *Wine & Food Handbook: Aide Memoir for the Sommelier & the Waiter*. Trans-Atlantic Publications, 2003.

Vandel, Philippe. Pourquoi. JC Lattes, 1993.

Wells, Patricia, *At Home in Provence: Recipes Inspired by Her Farmhouse in France*. Scribner, 1996.

Willan, Anne. *The Country Cooking of France*, Chronicle Books, 2007.

Yan, Martin. *Martin Yan's Asia*. KQED Books. 1997.

Young, Carolin, C. "The Sexual Politics of Cutlery," in *Feeding Desire: Design and the Tools of the Table 1500-2005*, Assouline Publishing, 2006

IF YOU HAVE ANY FOOD OR BEVERAGE STORIES TO SHARE PLEASE SEND TO AMBMELON@GMAIL.COM

Printed in Great Britain
by Amazon